BY CHAZ GOWER

# The Movies of
# AMY YIP

# The **MOVIES OF AMY YIP**
## by Chaz Gower

Special thanks to the Internet and to VHS and DVD for keeping the memory of Amy Yip in our hearts forever!

# Preface

I just want to point out that the rating system I use for the movies and TV shows in this book are WAY out of whack with U.S. Cinema, Chinese Cinema, and the rest of the World.

I'm rating Amy Yip's movies as an Amy Yip fan. And those ratings usually run along the lines of 'An underrated classic!' to 'Only for the Amy Yip completist.' When compared to, say, The Godfather Part 1, nothing here even comes close.

Nothing.

I'm just going to ASSUME that if you're reading this, then you already understand what the charm and unique style of Asian Cinema from this period of time was and so you already know how to take this content within the context of where it came from.

I'm not even going to try and edit that last paragraph.

Just enjoy it. There's a bigger story here, and I hope one day to tell it. But for now, here are the Movies of Amy Yip. MADE for your exploitation enjoyment.

# Why AMY YIP?

Why would I write a book about a Category III actress (a Hong Kong soft core nudie movie) from halfway around the world, that worked in the film business for only 3-5 years and has been retired now for 25 years?

That's a darn good question! But if you know who Amy Yip is, then you already know the answer.

Amy Yip Ji-Mei 葉子楣 was born July 10, 1965 (though some sources claim 1967, some 1966) in Hong Kong. She studied at the Kau Kam English College, and then took acting classes at the ATV channel, beginning a career in television.

Some believe this was when Amy had her breasts enhanced; though she claims they were enlarged due to her mother forbidding her to wear a bra.

She slowly gained popularity in Hong Kong movies in 1989, thanks to her large breast size (guesstimated anywhere from 36DD to 38F) on her small waisted, 5'3" frame. By 1990 she was one of the biggest stars in China, but by the end of 1992 was all but done with making movies.

But Amy wasn't just a pair of boobs, or two decades later I wouldn't be writing about her. There were a number of things that set her apart from the usual soft porn actresses of the business, that created an aura about her, and an interest in her, that still exists today.

Proof of that is, how the Chinese versions of TMZ, see her in public and still chase her down for interviews on a regular basis (she denies having any interest in returning to movies), and a quick search of the internet will reveal hundreds of pictures, along with websites and blogs, pretty much detailing the same sparse information we know about her.

And believe me, in trying to find collectible items that feature her from back then, I've seen (and sometimes paid) premium prices for some of these items.

So what was different about Amy?

Well, in no particular order, you have to start with her actual acting ability. If Anna Nicole Smith had made the huge splash on the American public consciousness that she did, knocked out a few movies and then retired, she still wouldn't be remembered for her acting. In fact, despite becoming a household name through tabloids and reality television, she's not really remembered at all for her acting ability, but rather her over the top persona.

Considering roughly half of Amy's movies were Category III films (including her two most infamous, 'Erotic Ghost Story' and 'Sex and Zen'), she played in almost as many comedies with a few dramas. And in them, her talent is noticeable; her ability to actually play the part, even some of the more simple parts she was at times given, is very evident.

And when the level of material is of a better quality, such as 1991's 'Queen of the Underworld', she actually shows superior talent, that should have put her into a higher level of respect. She was NOT just another pretty face.

Which brings us to the next point, she WAS a pretty face. Amy had a beautiful face, and a great smile, to go along with sad, dark eyes. It made for a great combination, as generally many of the Hong Kong actresses from this time seemed to go out of their way NOT to smile. (Maggie Cheung being an obvious exception, and she was probably the #1 Chinese actress superstar of the era.)

This combination of a beautiful smile, vulnerable eyes, large breasts, and tiny waist was enough to make her a star. Her actual talent was enough to transcend that. But Amy had another ace up her sleeve, either through coyness or shrewd calculation, that would build the anticipation of each new movie.

She never showed her nipples.

OTHER actresses in the movies would show their nipples (and more), but Amy somehow was afforded the courtesy to NOT have them exposed, the angle of the camera going to great creative lengths to NOT let you see them. This became known as the 'Yip Tease'.

The anticipation of each new movie would grow. Would this be the one where she does? It made her a HUGE star in China, as well as Taiwan, the Philippines, Korea, and Japan, where regular newspaper stories speculated about her life, her loves, her breasts (are they real or not?), and more; eventually taking their toll on Amy as she withdrew from the industry.

To her credit, she never showed them. At least not intentionally (we'll get to that). In all of the movies, all of the photo sessions, the Penthouse Magazine pictures, you never saw them. The story is that she had an amount that she'd accept to show them, but if it was true, she was in the wrong part of the world for anyone to accept it.

Amy would spend a few years touring those same countries where her popularity had boomed, in support of a music CD she would record (selling out concerts and making a great deal MORE than she did as an actress), before eventually settling down with her boyfriend and investing in area restaurants.

In recent years, she's been seen in public on occasion, always cordial to the rabid press, and always dispelling rumors of a comeback. Some of the rumors involve doing 1000 situps a day and drinking only green tea, and things of that nature, but when specifically asked, she always denies any interest.

It hasn't helped that Amy's longtime boyfriend Orthopedic Surgeon Sammy Lui has put off marriage for over 20+ years, and Amy was quoted as saying, "I did have the urge to get married in the past but the matter has been dragged on for way too long. I do feel a little bored hanging out with my boyfriend now. I think it's better for us both if we give each other space."

But they're still together even now.

Incidentally, in a 2006 interview, Amy stated, in regards to her most famous feature, "Long ago my waist was only 20 or 21 inches, so it made my chest look especially big. Actually, my chest only measures 36 inches, not 40 inches like some magazines exaggerated."

Finally pressed with if she would ever come back, Amy gave a resounding 'No!'

If there's a book about her life story or an autobiography in the works, it's LONG overdue. For now, this is the only book you'll find!

## The Television Years

Amy got her start in television (from what I've been able to find) in 1984, at the age of 17 (or 18 or 19) with **WONG CHAO CHUN** 王昭君. It's about one of the four legendary beauties in Chinese history, who go through great hardship and sacrifice to bring peace to the warlike times.

They've collected at least the first 12 (of 20) episodes, and I don't believe she had a very big part in it, as she's usually listed last in any credits I've found and usually not listed for it at all.

Following that she appeared in **The MAGIC BLADE** 天涯明月刀 TV Series, in 1985, and from the first episode, it looked like she had a more substantial role. Until she got killed near the end of that first episode! Such is the life of a new talent in the biz!

Still, it's interesting to see the 18-ish year old Amy in this early role, where she had to act... and not rely upon her physical charms.

The Magic Blade was originally a celebrated Gu Long wuxia novel, that was made into an exceptional Shaw Brothers film in 1976 (with Ti Lung and Lo Lieh).

From what I can tell, this TV series wasn't as celebrated, but it has it's cult following. Generally, fans of wuxia entertainment (ancient martial arts heroes) can be pretty picky, but as long as an effort is made toward tradition, it'll find it's audience.

They're maybe comparable to American Westerns in our culture, except that they've never really gone out of style in China.

Some of the battle scenes are pretty good, though there does tend to be a little more unrealistic flips and flying type stuff than I prefer. Some of the sword battles are decently staged, especially for TV in the mid-80's.

Near the end of the first episode, it almost looks like Amy gets <u>punched in the breasts</u> (something that would become a recurring theme in some of her movies), but I can't positively say...most likely her shoulder, though how that ends up killing her, is suspect.

Even though it was only one episode for her, this was a pretty big part early in

Amy's career, on the road to much bigger parts....

In my research, Amy also had a credited part in the 1985 ATV series **SAAM SAI YAN** 三世人 (Three People), which I couldn't find much information on. The intro and outro are on YouTube, but Amy isn't in either. It's the story of three women from different eras in Chinese history (Ming Dynasty, Republic of China War, and modern times). It ran for 25 episodes.

I really wish I could find the 1986, 20 episode **LIVING BUDDHA JI GONG** 濟公活佛 TV series, also with a 20 year old Moon Lee 李賽鳳.

Ji Gong was a Buddhist Monk in the 1100's China, who supposedly had supernatural powers and protected the poor and stood up to injustice. Unlike most Monk's, he also was known to drink, eat meat and chase women, which may have caused him some trouble at the time but, would eventually turn him into a major Chinese folk hero.

Sounds like the perfect adventure for Amy to be a part of!

A 1986 ATV series I know she's in is the 17 episode **SEPTEMBER EAGLES** drama based upon the Romantic Swordsman novels by Gu Long (Cologne). September
Eagles is the second installment.

The entire series was on Youtube at the time, and I found a translation of the novel on Wuxia.com to read/follow along.

Early on it's pretty violent and bloody with a fair amount of action, but it became more of a serious drama by the time that Amy shows up, though having a reading source made it actually an enjoyable drama to watch.

A drama full of lies, deceit, and hidden identities.

I would imagine Amy looks back on this period with some amount of sentimental value... these were classic, historic Chinese folk tales featuring some of their greatest legends. To be a part of it, had to be much more satisfying than playing a sexy android killer in Robotrix a few years later!

Amy plays Auntie Xin, one of Nanhai Niang-zi's beautiful maidens'. This is how Gu Long describes them in the novel (translated): "Two beautiful women dressed in white, as white as snow, stood at each side out of respect, showing off peerless grace and beauty, actually even more beautiful than the young, as the beauty was refined and inconceivable. They were Auntie Tie and Auntie Xin."

 Of course, there's a secret to their identity as well. Or is there? Tianpeng and Han Zhen travel thousands of miles to confront the mysterious 'Thousand Goddess of Mercy' Nanhai Niang-zi, and encounter these two at the palace.

Bonnie Ngai (Ngaji Chow-Va) plays the powerful sword eating Auntie Tie.

Amy fits right in here, her performance is as quality as anyone else's. Amy's character is verbally promiscuous, for 1986 TV anyway, and this may be her first character she plays to fit that category .

Of course Gu Long had no way of knowing of Amy Yip who would one day play Auntie Xin in the TV production, but I found it interesting that they left this (translated) part from the book out of the TV Series:

> *Auntie Xin looked at him and suddenly smiles, "My chest is also much more attractive than hers, do you believe me?"*
>
> *Yang Tian was astounded, the face became flushed, "I... I... "*
>
> *Auntie Xin charmingly smiled, "Later I will let you have a look, at that time you will believe me."*
>
> *Yang Tian's palpitation grew quicker.*
>
> *Auntie Xin said, "Now first you carry this person surnamed Ye."*
>
> *Yang Tian said, "This Ding... Ding girl?"*
>
> *Auntie Xin said, "He can walk with me."*
>
> *She kicked Ding Lin's foot, turning her head to Yang Tian and smiled, "As long as you act smart and help us well, mother will let you nurse later."*

Both Auntie Tie and Auntie Xin, two very central characters to the first arc of the story, are fierce and heartless, but Auntie Xin, who we are told is Auntie Tie's daughter, has a playful sensuality to her. When she starts to search Ye Kai, Yang Tian protests, that a man should do it since he is a man.

*Auntie Xin stared, "Why can't I search men? I like searching man's body, in particular, attractive man."*
*Yang Tian nipped his lips and closed his mouth.*
*Auntie Xin smiled, "If you are jealous, wait for a little while, and I will search you too."*

Not sure how it's actually said in the TV Series, but they do play out the scene. Unfortunately, Amy's character here also meets an unfortunate end.

Oh well, she made it through 4 episodes this time! Very much recommended!

Also in 1986, was the 20 episode '**Bride With White Hair**' ATV series. Also referred to as 'The Romance of the White Haired Maiden', it's somewhat based upon the 1957 wuxia novel Baifa Monü Zhuan by Liang Yusheng, Of course, the most famous version, was the 1993 film starring Brigitte Lin and Leslie Cheung.

It has some decent swordplay and fighting, enough to make up for the flying and stuff, but seems like pretty standard TV action. Amy plays Mang Chua-ha, and is relegated to a small part.

1987 began with a part in the 30 episode TV Series **Gung Chan** (Red Dust) 紅塵, which I couldn't find. But the

20 episode Series **Love Hong Kong** 香港情, I watched a few episodes of and it seems Amy is one of the stars... and she's pretty funny in it!

Amy plays a housewife with a comedic relationship to her husband, very American like, and if they ever subtitled it, I'd buy the collection in heartbeat.

I'm not making any judgement calls here, as it doesn't matter to me either way, but Amy's bust size in these episodes is less than impressive. Either they had them flattened down or... maybe the rumors are true? Over the years Amy

has let female reporters feel them, and obviously done love scenes where her male co-stars feel them, and they ALL say they're real, so...

But this was the point where, as the story goes, Amy decided she wanted to move into doing movies, and leave her TV career behind. The industry was booming, and Amy wanted to be a star.

Anyway based on just her TV career, there really wasn't anything that stood out about Amy, or that gives us any hint that she would skyrocket to stardom. Though her appearance in **Hong Kong Love**, is quality, it's not necessarily superstar quality.

It would be in the movie industry that she would become a superstar.


## OTHER TV APPEARANCES:

As Amy would get recognition through her movies and become a star, she of course, had other television appearances.

Promotional appearances, Interviews, Paparazzi footage; between 1990 - 1992, it seemed Amy was always everywhere!

One of her more interesting television appearances, floating around out there on You Tube, is a promotional appearance for Erotic Ghost Story from 1989.

It's a Chinese talk show, and along with co-stars Man Siu 文素, and Kamimura Kiyoko 貝塚里美 (the demon's innocent victim), they discuss the movie and especially AMY, as the hosts seem quite taken by her!

Worth checking out on youtube!

**WHO IS THE CRAFTIEST?** (1988)

奸人本色

Jian ren ben se

WHO IS THE CRAFTIEST? (1988) was a Hong Kong comedy directed by Poon Man-kit 潘文傑, and featuring our Amy in a small role.    From what I can gather, it had a one week run in the Hong Kong theaters from January 1st through the 7th and grossed  HK$3,193,219 (or roughly US $411,000). Which in Hong Kong is considered fair, especially for a small low budget comedy like this

It starred Bill Tung Biu 董驃 (Jackie Chan's 'Police Inspector 'Uncle' in many of his films), Ricky Hui Koon-Ying 許冠英 (Mr. Vampire),  Tiffany Lau Yuk-Ting 劉玉婷 (as 'Winnie'), Sammi Cheung Wai 張煒 as Kang Cheun, and Shirley Kwan Suet-Lai 劉玉婷 as one of the other club girls.

The cast competes with each other to see 'who can be the craftiest', trying to trick people and live a life of no work luxury. I watched an original language version of it, so there may be more to it than that, but I doubt it.

There's also a subplot involving a love triangle between the goofy Ricky Hui, the suave Sammi Cheung, and the cute Tiffany Lau, with the Hui character getting the bad end of the deal through most of the movie.

Apparently, Bill Tung's character, screws over someone and one of the friend's dies (the older mother character played by Tang Pik-wan 鄧碧雲), and they all gang up to bankrupt Bill Tung, before he gets his revenge, comedy style. It's fairly goofy and forgettable but has its fun moments.

Amy Yip's first scene features her in bed with Bill Tung, apparently after having sex. As they talk, she gets out of bed holding covers around her, revealing her back. Bill Tung makes an 'aids' comment and she is offended and starts to leave. Tung reminds her to 'take the money', but she scoffs at this and leaves.

She looks cute in this scene, but not all that much to separate her from the endless number of cuties in these type of movies, and it's not exactly an earth shattering role.

Her next scene is in the cabaret as she hangs out as one of Sammi Cheung's group. The gold party dress she wears makes her look elegant, but once again nothing here to separate her from anyone else.

She has a short scene on the other end of the phone when they're tricking Bill Tung's character, where she goes from her dress to a towel as the scene bounces back and forth, but you'll miss it if you blink.

Finally, she's a part of the group that exposes Bill Tung's character in the bar and sings their revenge to him. Or whatever. Some of the reviews online of this movie, make me wonder if I even saw the same film, but I was lucky to find a copy.

And the copy I did find was a VCD! I'd forgotten they even made those things! In case you don't remember them, VCD's or Video CD's look just like a DVD, but have the resolution qualities of a VHS. It was a cheap way to sell more copies of as many movies as they could. This movie is probably deserving of the format!

So it's not anything special, and probably for Amy Yip completionists only. And available out there still somewhere on VCD!

Amy had hit the big screen, even if we didn't see all that much of her!

Growing Pains
**INSPECTOR WEARS SKIRTS II**
(1989)
神勇飛虎霸王花
Shen yong fei hu ba wang hua

The Inspector Wears Skirts II was Amy Yip's first higher profile type of movie, where she had a decent role to play, and it gave her the initial exposure to start her career. Opening in Hong Kong theaters on January 28th, 1989 (running for about a month), it pulled in HK $18 million, one of the bigger hits of 1989. (#7 by my count)

Which is not bad, I mean, this is Hong Kong 1989: John Woo's 'The Killer', Chow Yun Fat, and Jackie Chan dominate the market (plus the last Aces Go Places). But, IWS2 actually did well, and provides

the bullet-proof jacket

some laughs (though not enough real action). And of course, Sandra Ng, does her usual goofiness, and Amy doing HER thing, you can see why it was popular.

All of the Inspector Wears Skirts movies are about the training of female military personnel. Sort of a Police Academy type of movie featuring women.

Amy shows up, about 6 minutes in, as a part of the new class of trainees, and immediately they're being hazed by Sandra Ng from the first movies' class.

Hazing follows in the barracks as they try to get settled in and then the cafeteria. Now, the cafeteria features the new girls and older girls squaring off with some decent fighting, and... Amy doing at least one of her own stunts - rolling back over a table!

They ALL get in trouble for it, so in retribution, they use the old shit in a flaming bag trick at night in the barracks - each of the new girls falling for it. Amy doesn't have her slippers on, so she uses

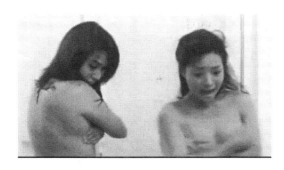

her backside to sit on it, then when realizing the trick, exclaims, "Lots of shit in my buttocks!"

Then there's the bulletproof vest.

Of course, Amy's doesn't fit her, as her breasts are too large, and this gets her into some trouble, but they come up with a solution later...

Anyway, when they all decide to have a party for Madam Wu's (Sibelle Hu) birthday, they invite some of the men soldiers from the base (Cult favorite Mars, of Jackie Chan's real life stunt team, being one of them). Amy's cleavage causes quite a stir, and at one point everyone breaks out into a choreographed dance scene... yeah, it's that kind of movie....

At about the 45 minute mark, there's a peeping tom shower scene, and Amy gives us her first 'Yip tease'.

Welcome to the wonderful world of making movies instead of TV! It's kind of

'Porky's-like', and not really all that revealing, and the 'peeper' certainly pays the price for his behavior.

Still, this kind of scene would be the first of many for Amy. She may not have known it at the time, but notice of her sexuality would quickly surpass her talent.

Sibelle Hu Hui-Chung 胡慧中 plays her usual straightforward no-nonsense self - and Sandra Ng Kwun-Yu 吳君如 takes massive abuse and makes funny faces.

Stanley Fung Sui-Fan 馮淬帆 also plays his usual type character in it as well, but Billy Lau Nam-Kwong 樓南光 gets most of the male directed abuse.

Jackie Chan 成龍 was the producer on this, but I'm not even sure what that means, as it neither resembles a Jackie Chan movie or has him in it. Maybe his name helped at the Box Office? Like I said, this one has it's moments. I'm still waiting on a Blu-ray copy to come out as I have yet to see a really good transfer on DVD.

## Oh By the Way...

In between Amy grabbing attention from the IWS2 movie, she also had a few smaller roles leading up to more prominent parts...

### Heart to Hearts 三人世界 (1988)

Listed as 'Girl at Alex's Party', Amy is in only one scene and....and doesn't do much...Knocking out HK $24 million (#105 on Hong Kong's All Time Box Office) and running from 8/25/1988 to 10/14/1988, it may have been one of her lamest movies, but it was one of her highest grossing!

### Mr. Canton and Lady Rose 奇蹟 (1989)

Jackie Chan once made some disparaging comments about Amy Yip (essentially saying she was ugly). As far as I know, the big nosed horn dog only worked with her on this one movie so... who knows? Maybe she told him no?

Judging by the seconds she's in this movie, that's MY guess! Maybe my least favorite of the mid-career Chan flicks, it did HK $34 million (#50 on Hong Kong's All Time Box Office) in the middle of June 1989. Two of Amy's biggest movies (and smallest parts) back 2 back!

**GHOST FEVER** 鬼媾人 **(1989)** was released in Hong Kong on April 20th, 1989, running for 19 days and pulling in a respectable HK $5.9Million.

Directed by Lau Shut-Yue 劉仕裕 , it's the story of a married guy (played by Director Wong Jing! 王晶), who moves into a haunted house with his wife, Pat Ha Man Jik 夏文汐) and one night while she's at the hospital, he has an affair with a pretty ghost (the lovely Rosamund Kwan Chi-Lam 關之琳).

Problem is, she falls in love with him, and he stands her up, so her family (also ghosts), featuring mean older sister (Eliza Yue Chi-Wai 于芷蔚 ), decide they want revenge!

Amy's character is named Nancy and is just another girl who is a part of this silliness. She gets startled by one of the guys when they first investigate the house and joins the group later for a card game, and in between whatever non-funny boredom is going on here, joins the group again for dinner that night.

Her possession and levitation scenes aren't bad during that dinner, but her final scene is, again as a secretary, witnessing the Jing blood splatter behind his office window, as the sister ghost (who SHE can't see) is attacking Jing.

It IS or at least COULD have been a classic Amy Yip horror clip, as she looks quite sexy walking by and then stopping to unknowingly watch, and then screaming, as the blood splatters on the window, obscuring our girl - BUT, they botch the shot! A director with a little more of an artistic touch could've made this a real gem!

Amy's next movie **LOST SOULS** 富貴開心鬼 **(1989)**, ran from August 9th, 1989 to August 23rd, 1989, (two whole weeks this time!) and did a respectable HK $5.6 Million. Directed by David Lai Dai-Wai 黎大煒 (Fong Sai Yuk II), and starring Bill Tung Biu 黎大煒 (again), who is up to some silly scheme that's par for a HK comedy of this type.

David Wu Dai-Wai 吳大維 , as the 'boyfriend' is an uptight businessman who has our Amy constantly trying to seduce him. Maybe this subplot was added to spice things up a bit because the rest of the movie is lame-o.

If some of Amy's small early roles seemed to be unaware of her, or unwilling to feature her most famous body part(s), Lost Souls dives right in from the start. Her first scene features her in a skin tight, white blouse with a  far south plunging neckline, and she uses it to try and seduce David Wu's character.

After getting brushed off, she returns to drop the blouse down on one revealing shoulder, only to get rebuffed again, when Wu's character shows her a picture of his girlfriend.

I realize, Yip is known for her breasts, but her acting in this scene is very natural and playful. Sure, it's what you'd figure she might be good at, but I've seen plenty of attractive women in movies who COULDN'T act, and come across as stiff and boring in a scene like this. Yip is anything but, and really has a warmth to her that is noticeable and unique from the endless number of cuties that appear in these HK comedies.

Her second scene... well, if there was any question of the film makers understanding of Amy's soon to be famous assets, it's squelched right here.

She gets out of a car, pretending to be blind in a skin tight black muscle shirt,

with a waist cinch that accentuates her as well as possible. She meets two associates as they plan to mug the Wu character as Amy sneaks in some kisses.

They even make a boob joke, as Amy tries to hide behind a pillar, not realizing her breasts stick out to reveal her still. She ends up getting smacked by some old Kung Fu guy, which seems a little harsh.

After that, it's not until the closing credits outtakes that she has anything to do....

## MR. SUNSHINE 開心巨無霸 (1989)

was released August 1st ,1989 for 15 days (August 16th, 1989) bringing in HK $3,936,619 , once again decent for a small HK comedy.

Directed by HK actor Philip Chan Yan-Kin 陳欣健 and starring plump comedian Kent Cheng Jak-Si 鄭則仕, it's a pretty standard Hong Kong comedy.

Amy plays 'May', who works in a department store doing jumping exercises on a mini trampoline behind a screen that shows her silhouette. I have no idea how that's a job (hey, it was the 80's), but Amy is pretty much the perfect girl for the part! It's a small role, but a memorable one in that it had viewers thinking, 'Who is THAT girl?'

So, the store manager (Richard Ng) hires Maria Cordero to be an additional exerciser (for some reason), but she quickly tires out, despite Amy's friendly support. Kent ends up exercising FOR HER behind the screen (even wearing a bra), so she won't lose the job. The only explanation is: It's a Hong Kong Comedy.

There is one scene of a robbery in a doctor's office that has some humorous gags to it, but overall, besides Amy's part, it's fairly dull.

**DOCTOR'S HEART** 救命宣言 **(1990)** was released sometime in 1990 (can't seem to find a specific date), and appears to be some sort of ER type of drama. All I had was an un-dubbed/un-subtitled copy, but it looked to be fairly entertaining.

It certainly has its share of stars in it: The multi-talented Simon Yam 任達華, wearing glasses and a scowl, plays a hard nosed medical administrator; Mark Cheng Ho-Nam 鄭浩南 as the heartthrob doctor with 'turmoil' or whatever; his friend, the silly Lowell Lo Koon-Ting 盧冠廷 (who has somehow managed to be Yip's boyfriend here), Bill Tung Biu 黎大煒 (yet again!), and Michelle Reis 李嘉欣, as the love interest torn between Yam and Cheng.

There is some humor in it, though it gets all heavy in the last act. Once again some humor is thrown in, as they stop Yam from turning off the power on an unauthorized surgery going on!

Our Amy plays a regular nurse, who's part seems to grow as the story does, and she actually gets a fair amount of screen time here. And she's quite cute in her fairly unglamorous role. Then again, this practically a TV movie.

She does get <u>punched in the boob</u> by an unruly kid patient and wears a nice party dress that shows off her cleavage, but other than that, it's a fully dressed, NORMAL part for Amy. And she's good.

These were all movies she made before things really exploded, but the 80's were over now and Amy's star was growing!

## The 90's are here!

**TO SPY WITH LOVE** 小心間諜 **(1990)** came out at the end of March 1990 and ran through the first week of April, softly landing in at HK $3.4MIL (US $440,000). No surprise, as they kill off Amy's character in the first 15 minutes!

Ama starts off the movie running through the night time streets trying to get away from some young creeps, going into a club until finally getting shot! Before she expires, she leaves a secret microchip tape inside Terry Robin Kwan's 泰迪羅賓 vehicle (a yellow van that transports the all-female band he manages - Terry and the Playgirls).

This is HIS movie, which doesn't make it any easier to watch. There are a few funny moments, but really a lot of silly nonsense before we finally get the sexy Sibelle Hu Hui-Ching 胡慧中 squaring off with the equally sexy Nina Li Chi 利智 (Jet Li's wife). That final battle isn't a masterpiece of martial arts, but it's kinda fun, kinda sexy, and one of the only decent highlights in an otherwise boring movie.

Ultimately it could've used more Amy!

## JAILHOUSE EROS (1990)
監獄不設防

Jian yu bu she fang

An early Category III winner (HK $5.8 Million) that should be a B-movie classic. It combined all of the elements of what the Hong Kong market loves: silly comedy, gross horror, and sex.

I'm sure Amy Yip didn't start out thinking Category III (the equivalent of a U.S. 'R' rating) would be her stepping stone to fame, but.... in Taiwan, Japan, and other Southeast Asian countries, additional nudity was added to the movie, and the reaction to it was even more financially rewarding.

On top of that, it's cult status on VHS and DVD over the years have shown it to be a movie far more popular than it's initial HK Box Office totals! (Even though it's still not that easy to find.)

A conservative and shy HK mainstream really hadn't embraced Category III movies in 1990. HK $5.9 Million is decent for a Cat III, and even respectable by regular movie standards in China, but it would be a Category that Amy would lead to new heights!

There was nudity and violence in Chinese movies, but these were small parts of the story. Category III movies have a story, but the focus is much greater on the sex and violence, sometimes going way over the top.

The movie opens with Loletta Lee's character trying to escape from the prison by climbing down an outside drain pipe . She drops her music box and when she goes to reach for it, she falls and dies. We then see a black magic priest of some sort, take her name tag and perform a ritual, and encase it inside of a small statue.

15 years later we meet a female prisoner of the same jail, Blackie (Joanna Chan Pui-San 陳佩珊(1) who is also trying to escape, having somehow put together a rope made of the strongest toilet paper in the world. But as her  escape plan is all a dream and she's brought back to the world inside the jail

by the square jawed Yan Hiu-Yee（殷曉儀 exceptional in her only known film role) who immediately starts pushing her around, as her cell block gang joins in to help.

We then meet the rival cell block group of girls, featuring our own Amy as 'Chesty', and an amazing Maggie Cheung look-a-like in Wong Mei-Wa 王美華 wearing wire rimmed glasses, but displaying a fierce fighting style... they come to Blackie's aid, not so much to save her, as you can tell they just don't like the other girls, and... as they complain about Blackie waking them up, Chesty mocks one of them for her own 'night time noises - humping her pillow) and then all hell breaks loose.

Which leads to footage added for the Taiwan cut, or removed for the Chinese version (whichever it was) featuring torn smocks (some of these girls strategically don't wear underwear) and even a bit more violence... Blackie wants nothing to do with it, and 'Big Sister' played by Maria Cordero 瑪利亞 tries to break it up, but ends up getting the blame.

'Rough Prison Guard' played by Ha Chi-Chun 夏志珍 (and played to perfection, I might add) comes in and starts busting some of them over the head, and assumes unfairly that 'Big Sister' is behind it all and takes her to solitary.

Next, we meet the comic relief of the movie in the stuffy, uptight Inspector, played by Stanley Fung Sui-Fan 馮淬帆 as he brings in 3 immature young male workers to help fix up the prison: Dickson Lee Ga-Sing 李家聲 , Cheng Kwan-Chi 鄭君熾 and Lawrence Lau Sek-Yin 劉錫賢 as 'Fatty' (of course).

They have other ideas though and as they start to unload their equipment outside, it's just as the guard is marching the cellblock group right past them. She reminds them (while paying no attention to what's going on) to ignore the boys, but it's the girls who whistle at THEM, creating a competition between the two groups to see who can get noticed most.

The girls quickly realize none of them can compete with 'Chesty's' chest and so they bend over and start shaking their butts, causing Chesty and her group to do the same, much to the delight of the boys. It turns into a fight though, complete with more torn smocks and nudity. But 'Rough Prison Guard' comes to break it up, she accidentally gets a stripe of spray paint across her face - the fury of her expression is priceless.

As punishment, she lines the girls up and takes great delight in hosing them down with a high powered fire hose. If you're expecting high art here, you'll be sorely disappointed as this is pretty much the expected women in prison type of storyline. It just has more genre's added!

It's interesting to see a young Amy in these scenes and she really stands out. Even though she's not listed as a 'star' in this movie, it's very clear that the director is not only aware of her special attributes, but her charm and likable screen presence as well.

Next we learn that 'Rough Prison Guard' has a secret...a boyfriend who she sneaks in at night to use for her own pleasure (SHE finishes, he doesn't). But in the midst of roughly arguing they break open the statue (as the boyfriend leaves), releasing Loletta Lee's ghost, who startles 'Rough Prison Guard' into falling down and hitting her head, instantly killing her.

So, this ghost (the girl from the intro) can only be free, if she helps someone else escape, or something and then there's the ghost of 'Rough Prison Guard', who comes back to try and kill everyone.... yeah, it's what you'd expect from this kind of mish-mash of genre's. It gets a bit confusing at times.

Meanwhile, Amy and the other girls are just as dead set on getting laid as the 3 goofy boys, but their kitchen rendezvous doesn't work out. Amy again oozes with innocent sexuality in this scene, but in subtle behavior as well, because it features comedy and fear (of getting caught).

We then get the cafeteria scene, featuring not only the best all out brawl (with more torn smocks and nudity), the return and again removal of 'Big Sister', and the first real appearance of Ghost Loletta to Blackie (no one else can see her). This leads to a real panic as Blackie freaks out, freaking everyone else out.

Of course during the brawl, Amy gets a nice chunk bit out of the front of her smock, exposing some cleavage. All of this happens in the first 30 minutes of the movie!

It's a Women in Prison movie so naturally there's a shower scene, and this is Amy's first real nude scene (in as far as what a Amy Yip nude scene is).

I don't want to fixate on it, but it IS a much more revealing scene than her group shower scene in Inspector Wears Skirts 2. Amy is showering and talking to the girl in the stall next to her. We see them both nude from behind (from the waist up), but Amy can't help but give us a large helping of side boob, as she casually chats.

And this of course would add to her already growing legend and mystique. It isn't something I created - it's what happened at the time!

Now is hoping for a remastered Blu-Ray version really too much to ask for? With deleted scenes?

Something better than a VCD...

Amy has some interesting parts later in the movie; she's bound to a chair (along with Blackie - it's part of the 'ritual') in a specific way to accentuate her boobs; and supernaturally <u>swallows a whole nightstick</u> (another recurring theme - phallic mouth stuffing), and then has a lip lock with Dickson Lee Ga-Sing 李家聲 that swings him around the room. When she finally spits up the nightstick it explodes which is when the ghost of 'Rough Prison Guard' is resurrected! And boy does she look creepy!

Amy has one other funny part, where her boobs won't fit all the way inside the circle of protection a medium has created for them and she has to keep pushing back farther, much to everyone's dismay.

The special effects are what you'd expect from a 1990 Chinese low budget movie.

An underrated classic that again accentuates not only Amy's sexuality but also her charm and comedy acting. Good fun! Sort of like a low budget independent movie, where they just threw stuff in to it because it sounded cool. Which to me, always sounds like a good idea.

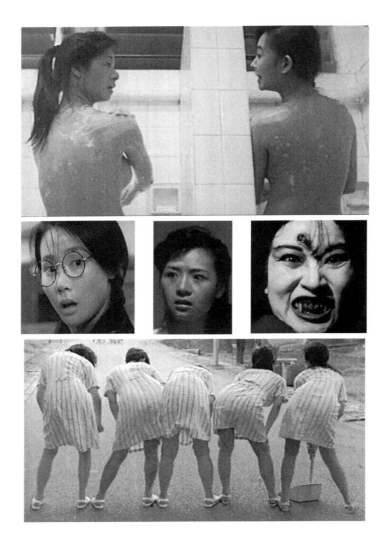

**MY NEIGHBORS ARE PHANTOMS** 嘩鬼住正隔籬 **(1990)** (it should be My Neighbors are VAMPIRES, but whatever) came out in Hong Kong theaters April 26th, 1990 and ran for a whole 8 days until May 4th, pulling in a decent HK $4.9Million. Written and produced by Wong Jing 王晶 (and directed by Lau Shut-Yue 劉仕裕) it's your pretty standard Wong Jing silly mix of genres.

Nat Chan Pak-Cheung 陳百祥 is a bumbling cop (he's always a bumbling something in these movies), who along with his top cop partner (and magician?) Chung Fat 鍾發 take on some small time crooks who've stolen a haunted picture of a family who are alive in the picture!

It falls into the hands of Charlie Cho Cha-Lee 曹查理 (who could double for Wong Jing himself) a wealthy peeping tom, who unwittingly releases the ghostly family.

Chingmy Yau Suk-Ching 邱淑貞 plays one of the pretty spied upon female neighbors (along with cutie Mui Siu-Wai 梅小惠 ), so at least it kind of has that going for it, and Sharia Cheung Man 張

敏 is beautiful, as the ghost that wants to be human again for...Love!

We eventually learn they're all vampires and the rest of her vampire family is made up of sister Mondi Yau Yuet-Ching 邱月清, brother Sherman Wong Jing-Wa 黃靖華 , and dad Felix Lok Ying-Kwan 駱應鈞.

Amy's part starts out, playing a nagging girlfriend (at least its a new part) to that goofy Nat Chan Pak-Cheung. To his credit, he looks absolutely miserable when she's berating him.

Amy actually punches out Chung Fat with her boobs (wearing a silky red blouse, that I swear shows off her fully erect nipples), but afterwards, Chung does a magic trick - inflating her boobs, and then deflating them - using his mind and two glasses - yeah, it's THAT kind of silly. Gee, thanks for the movie part, Wong Jing!

Amy shows up later, as Nat takes his ghost out for a romantic dinner, but she can't SEE her, so she thinks Nat is nuts. Ghost Sharia starts playing tricks on Amy, sending a flying chicken wing into her mouth (see what I mean about a recurring theme ...), and possessing her into a sexual frenzy which she tries to take out on another patron.

After Amy and the two female neighbors try tricking the Vampire into outing herself, they enlist the aid of the magician cop Chung. Vampire sister Mondi, turns out has a mighty long tongue and despite being held in place by the group, manages to undo Amy's top!... I guess even vampire's want to see Amy's breasts!

In the Vampire realm, Nat changes into a Bruce Lee fighter (complete with yellow fight suit with black stripe) - yeah, it's Wong Jing here...This movie is neither scary or all that funny, and really if not for Amy being in it, kind of a waste of time.

Next, Amy had a very small cameo (and I mean SMALL) appearance in the Sammo Hung Kam-Bo 洪金寶 produced action flick **SHE SHOOTS STRAIGHT** 皇家女將 (1990) directed by Corey Yuen Kwai 元奎 and starring his future wife Joyce Godenzi 高麗虹.

Besides Yuen, who is one of the most well- known action choreographers, the film featured a bevy of Hong Kong legends and stars.

It ran in Hong Kong theaters in April of 1990, pulling in HK $9.9Million, a nice haul, even though Amy's in it very briefly. As in VERY brief.

I watched an original language version of it with no dubs or subtitles (though a very nice copy) and, it's pretty stylish (and violent!) through most of it. In the middle, it gets bogged down with some sappy stuff, but when it kicks, it kicks hard.

Seriously, as lame as all the drama is in it, the action is really good. Which of course, you'd expect from a Sammo movie.

Amy's part, is as an extra, in a meeting room, seated, where they show her for about 5 seconds. It's not sexy, interesting, or even really necessary. But I included it here because she's in it!

Joyce Godenzi 高麗虹 is bad ass as usual (and sexy too) - how she didn't become a huge star during this time is beyond me. And you can't go wrong with Yuen Wah 元華 as the bad guy.

Also, Sandra Ng Kwun-Yu 吳君如 (from the Inspector Wears Skirts movies) and Carina Lau 劉嘉玲 play cop sisters to Godenzi.

The final showdown between Godenzi and kickboxer Agnes Aurelio 阿金內斯·奧雷裏奧 is a highlight of not only the film but of women fight scenes in general. It might be, for looks AND fight talent, one of the better onscreen showdowns.

As 'Girls with Guns movies go, this one is aces. Well worth checking out, though not for Amy Yip.

Amy was becoming a star, as the Hong Kong press was more than happy to concentrate on putting her top-heavy pictures in every magazine they could.

She'd been in some legitimate films of higher quality (as Hong Kong films go) and some of questionable artistic value; and it had made her a known celebrity.

It was nothing compared to what came next.

## Becoming a Star!
# EROTIC GHOST STORY (1990)

聊齋艷譚

Liu jai yim taam

**EROTIC GHOST STORY 聊齋艷譚 (1990)** is the movie that really exploded Amy Yip into stardom. It may have to do with her lesbian scene, her sex scene, and the fully nude scene she has in the movie (minus any nipple or naughty bit, other than her butt crack - the 'Yip tease' phrase was probably officially born here). They promoted this movie heavily on Hong Kong TV with appearances and interviews and it paid off.

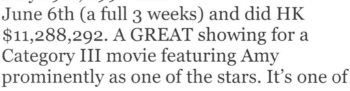

Still, being a Category III movie, it ran from May 19th, 1990 thru June 6th (a full 3 weeks) and did HK $11,288,292. A GREAT showing for a Category III movie featuring Amy prominently as one of the stars. It's one of the highest grossing Category III films ever.

Directed by Nam Lai-Choi (Story of Rikki) and also starring Man Siu 文素, and Kudo Hitomi 工藤瞳 (in her only full listed Chinese mainstream role), along with Amy as three beautiful 'fox fairies'. If they behave and do good deeds, they will eventually be granted immortality.

Into their lives comes the scholarly (Ng Ming) Tan Lap-Man 單立文, who one by one seduces each of the ladies, as they try and deceive each other about what they're up to.

When they go to confront him together, they find out he is a Demon, Wu-Tang, the God of Carnal Desire. So they gang up to fight him. Some compare it to 'The Witches of Eastwick' but set in old-time China.

But EGS is more of an erotic HORROR story, as there are no ghosts, though it makes up for it in the 'eroticism' part, with some gratuitous nudity you maybe wouldn't even see in an R rated U.S. mainstream release. Kudo Hitomi, in what appears to be her only Chinese role I'm aware of (she has a small part in EGS2), has a 'legs wide open' scene that really surprised me. She was a former Japanese AV model but had become an adult entertainer, and adult film actress the year before.

The movie starts out with the three sisters, named Fa-Fa (Amy Yip), Fei-Fei (Kudo Hitomi) and Pai So So (Man Siu), depending on which translation you read, wandering about the old-time China countryside.

Fei-Fei (Kudo Hitomi) stops by a small merchants tea stand (run by longtime Hong Kong actor Sai Gwa-Pau), where she battles off the advances of two local hoodlums.

They run to get help and soon a gang of five of them are out for revenge when they come upon Fa-Fa (Amy Yip) out in the countryside. They're ready to all take a go at her when Amy brings out 4 'sisters' from the wilderness so that everyone has a partner.

It's a trick of course, as in mid-frolic the 'sisters' all suddenly become decomposing corpses, scaring the hell out of the hoodlums and sending them running off with their pants half down. It's a pretty funny scene.

As much as I believe this movie is the one that made Amy a BIG star, and of course the sexuality of it helped, it's this opening scene that served her quite nicely as well.

She's dressed in a layered, sheer, multiple shade of lavender, somewhat traditional Chinese gown with her hair pulled up in a unique erected braid. There isn't a large amount of focus on her breasts here, but rather the beauty of her face, making the announcement that she is more than just 'The Big Bust Queen' (as the Chinese Press call her), but rather, a complete exquisite beauty altogether.

Pai So So (Man Siu) meanwhile, wanders into town, where she visits a statue of WuTang, the deity of fertility. A local woman tells her that any woman who is 'barren' and then blessed by him will become pregnant. She has a strange moment with the statue where she becomes overwhelmed and quickly leaves. She runs into a Taoist Priest named Hsuan Kuei (Lam Chung 林聰), who she blows off, but who then shows up on her path back home.

He warns her that she is an 'accomplished vixen' in human form, and her lust for WuTang will lead to trouble, and she needs to repent. Prideful, she starts to battle the old man with magic, but he retreats and tells her if there is trouble she can contact him at Pi Tan Falls. Hmm...

The three sisters convene in their beautiful home where Pai So So reminds them that they have 36 more days until they are immortal, and they need to beware of those who might try to steer them wrong and ruin it for them. Despite the obvious foreshadowing, they all agree.

The noisy neighbor Mrs. Wong stops by (played by former HK model, and one of my favorites Ha Chi-Chun 夏志珍 - she was 'Rough Prison Guard' in Jailhouse Eros) and makes note of no men living with them in their large house and offering her courtesy if needed from next door. She then grills her henpecked husband, before agreeing to sex that lasts all of ten seconds! She's NOT happy about it.

The sisters meditate before Buddha, and a vision of what they desire appears in Fa-Fa (Amy Yip) and Fei-Fei's (Kudo Hitomi) separate fantasies. Lust for a man!

That night Fa-Fa (Amy Yip) is restless and can not sleep... she pulls her full-sized pillow close to her, but it is not enough... Amy looks amazing here. Sexy, yes, but more than that...

She wanders outside where she sees her sister Fei-Fei's (Kudo Hitomi) bathing nude in the moonlight. Amy watches her begin to pleasure herself, and it excites her. She interrupts by splashing the water, and at first, Fei-Fei is startled, but she quickly smiles as Amy disrobes and joins her.

Say what you want about the technical quality of Hong Kong movies sometimes, but this is a really wonderfully erotic scene. Sure, if that's not your thing then, why are you reading this book?

The Yip tease is in full effect here, as they embrace and... enjoy each other, but it's incredibly hot!

Pai So-So wakes up and walks outside to see them, a stern look upon her face that momentarily lightens... she starts to walk forward to join? Stop them? But simply shakes her head and goes back inside to the Buddha statue to pray.

The next morning Pai So-So wakes up and walks into the forest where she sees

three swordsmen dressed in black chasing a frightened traveler. She steps between them and when they threaten her she uses magic to violently brush them away, sending them running.

She turns the poor 'Scholar' over and immediately is smitten by his face, politeness and his humility (as all other men seemed to be sex-crazed fiends), and helps him home. While he is changing, she uses magic to organize and clean his home. She talks him into letting her visit and buy food and cook for him.

When she returns home very late in the day, the other two sisters are full of worry in waiting for her. She lies to them and says she's just been out walking, but they see her preening in the mirror, and then dressing brightly and leaving again the next day.... so Fei-Fei follows her.

She watches as Pai So-So waits on him, but when she leaves Fei-Fei makes her move and goes into his hut. She peeks through a hole in a tarp and accidentally sees the Scholar showering, and her gasp and fall alerts him...He admonishes her for 'peeping' and sends her away crying.

Amy is furious to hear about this and sets out to confront him with a small sword. They end up wrestling to the ground, and before you know it they are overcome with passion!

Look, I know it's a Category III movie, and it's about... sex. Exploitation. I get it. But this scene is really, really well done. It's symbolic, beautifully shot, and... sure there's simulated sex, but... why does that have such a stigma in society to it?

No one has an issue with, "Hey did you see that one movie where the guy got his head blown off? Wasn't that cool? It looked so real!" Why is violence so applauded, and sexuality, so... frowned upon? This is well done erotica and deserves its due.

So Amy gets back home, feeling rather guilty, she deceives Fei-Fei into thinking she punished the Scholar. Of course, Fei-Fei is curious, so she goes back to see.

Mistaking the scratches all over his body from his lovemaking with Amy, she thinks he was tortured and takes pity on him, agreeing to nurse his wounds. This leads to one of the more controversial scenes in the movie where they end up making love. We see lots of close-ups of

Fei-Fei's pubic region, but that isn't all...Fei-Fei spreads her legs open wide, as in wide open, showing off more than you'd normally see in an R rated American mainstream movie, and even more than I think you'd normally see in even a Category III movie in 1990!

You don't see any penetration or anything like that, in fact, the scene is actually a LOT hotter than what you'd see in actual porn. And certainly better than some of Kudo Hitomi's porn, which at later points devolved into some harder S&M stuff.

When Pei So-So shows back up at the Scholar's hut, she discovers a hairpin and is distressed that he has another girl - when she finds out its Fei-Fei AND Amy, she smacks the Scholar to the ground, where his bare foot becomes visible. Overcome with desire she faints and he carries her to his bed and they make love.

There are some fairly eyebrow-raising moments here as well, with where she has her hands on what looks like his aroused crotch... but... three really tasteful well-done sex scenes.

Later the three sisters at dinner try and talk about what has happened... they each apologize to the other just as the Scholar walks in and says, "I'm here!" They share a happy group hug.

This is followed by the four of them prancing in a field together (How does Amy stay in that dress?), sharing a sensual meal together, and finally sharing a bath together in the same spring that Fei-Fei and Amy were in. BUT, this bath is spied upon by Mr. Wong!

It makes him horny and run to his wife, but she wants no part of him and his 10-second sex and kicks him in the groin. So she goes next door to inquire about their 'guest'. She then lectures them on their promiscuity and promises to tell the village leader about what's going on.

After she leaves they decide they must tell the Scholar he has to leave, otherwise they may not be able to become immortal in 36 days. He takes it fairly well, and mentions someone must have swayed their thinking, but gives each of them a peach to eat... and as each of them spits out the pit, Mrs. Wong next door begins to spit out fruit! He then performs some kind of voodoo ritual on a pineapple that has Mrs. Wong all kinds of horny - she begs her husband to do it to her.

He says he hasn't recovered from getting kicked in the groin, but she rips his clothes off and forces herself on him!

We then see the Scholar growing old in his hut, as he creates a butterfly out of magic and requests that it finds a woman

soon or he'll grow old and die.... it finds a woman down by the river and she follows the butterfly back to the Scholar, who puts a spell on her, as she happily undresses for him he laughs out loud at his find.

Meanwhile, Fei-Fei wakes up with fox hair on her chest! (And a fox head in the mirror!) She screams to her sisters that she's worried she's changing back to her original form, and they discover they too have the same hairy scare! They figure he must have used magic to lower their defenses, and now they're changing back. So they go to confront him.

What a surprise they find!

Peeking through that same hole filled tarp they see him changing into his three headed demon form and literally tear the skin from his female victim's body. Scared out of their minds they run to plot what to do next.

Pei So-So goes to Hsuan Kuei (The Taoist Priest from early on in the movie) to ask for help. He gives her some advice, (Magic beats power or something), and the three sisters create a 'voodoo doll', and begin their assault on the demon.

It's a pretty astonishing finale, as once they think they have him beat he comes back in Human Form and hypnotizes them, has them undress (We see Amy's naked behind for the first time), ready to bed all three, when....

The Taoist Priest shows up, snapping them out of the spell and then destroying the demon for good. The three sisters thank him for his help and then he flies off, and... wait, that's the end? No Prologue or anything?

The special effects are, of course not great at times, but if you're watching this in the spirit of when and where it was made, you'll be ok.

Personally, I love this movie. The wire stunts are few, thankfully, and the action (though sparse) was decent, the women are beautiful, and each scene is necessary for the overall movie so it moves along at a nice pace.

A classic of Hong Kong Cinema!

**Oh, By the Way....**

**NOTE:** In many online sources, you'll see the date for Erotic Ghost Story listed as 1987. This is incorrect.

Most likely it's being confused with Producer Tsui Hark's **A Chinese Ghost Story** 倩女幽魂 **(1987)**, starring Joey Wong Cho-Yin 王祖賢 and Leslie Cheung Kwok-Wing 張國榮, which most certainly is NOT a Category III movie, but was up for some awards in Hong Kong that year.

**ALSO:** Amy Yip has a short cameo in **A TALE FROM THE EAST** 漫畫奇俠 **(1990)** (June 28-July 6th HK $3MIL), and when I say short, I mean like 10 seconds.

She plays herself, signing an autograph for a fan.

Had her star risen that fast where she was already playing herself in a movie cameo?

Apparently so....

## Paparazzi!

If you think the Paparazzi are a new phenomenon, man, they were brutal in Southeast Asia back in the 90's. Between the triads and the magazines, it's a wonder anyone wanted to be in the business!

Some scuttlebutt from early in Amy's career:

*Lianhe Wanbao's senior correspondent Khoon Siew Kin recalled with amusement how Amy once strutted around in a loose white T-shirt, visibly bra-less.*

*It was Amy's first visit to Singapore to shoot a movie scene with Hong Kong actress Michelle Reis at the National Skin Centre in 1989.* (That would've been 'Doctor's Heart' in late 1989/early 1990 - my own edit)

*Then, Amy was still unknown in Singapore.*

*Miss Khoon said: 'I was talking to Michelle and Amy just kept walking up and down in front of us, her chest bouncing, trying to get media attention.'*

*They met again in 1991. By then Amy was such hot property that she was*

invited to perform at the Singapore Indoor Stadium.

This time, Miss Khoon remembers being 'poked' several times in the chest by Amy during an interview.

'She's a nice person and you can ask her anything. I even asked her if her breasts were fake.

'She said they're real and that I'd know by poking her there. Of course, I didn't dare to, but she kept poking my chest after that.'

As hard-hitting news as that may be, this article from the San Fransisco Chronicle, dated April 22, 1992, puts the times in better perspective:

*Daily Notebook Section. David W. Chen  Associated Press*

## MOB DOG HONG KONG FILM INDUSTRY

*Triads make violence part of real life*

*Film producer Choi Chi Ming stepped out of an elevator last week and into a hail of .38-caliber bullets fired by two men dressed in security guard uniforms. But this time, no one yelled "Cut!"*

*Police believe Choi was gunned down by Hong Kong's notorious triads, or organized crime gangs. If that's true, Choi's death would be the latest act of real-life violence in the business of make-believe.*

*TRIAD ATTACKS*

Last year, police recorded six triad-related attacks on film industry employees, including three in two days that left one man dead and another with a gunshot wound in the neck. Choi's death Thursday is believed to be linked to his alleged involvement in narcotics trafficking.

A senior police officer, speaking on condition of anonymity, said Choi had close links to heroin traffickers in the Netherlands and used his production company, as a front to launder drug profits.

As such, the shooting highlights the nexus between Hong Kong's underworld and its multimillion-dollar movie industry, which dominates box offices through SE Asia.

"People in the film industry don't mind triads, but they do mind triads who don't play the rules of the game," said legislator Rita Fan, who chairs the British colonial government's Security Panel and advocates tougher anti-triad statutes.

Triads long have pressured actors, producers and directors to pay protection money and act in triad-

*backed movies at reduced rates. Film crews also must pay up to thousands of dollars in "protection fees" to prevent hooligans from breaking expensive equipment.*

**"I have been threatened to make movies I didn't want to make.**

*These bad people will do anything to get money," said Amy Yip, Hong Kong's soft-porn queen. (They call porn, what we view as 'R' rated movies in the U.S.) "Everybody is very concerned, like one big family. We must stop this."*

Of course, all of this type of thing led to one of the more ugly rumors about Amy: "Buxom starlett Amy Yip Chi-mei was reportedly raped for not agreeing to appear in a production."

This rumor was specifically aimed at her appearance in 'Sex and Zen', one of her last movies, that features her most 'infamous' and revealing nude scenes. But the truth of the matter is... if you look closely, it's a body double for the parts shot under the hot tub water. You never see Amy's face with that body.

Even though it's still Amy's most revealing and sexual scene, the skin tone doesn't match up with the underwater body.

She may have quit the industry because she was FORCED to do this movie... but she was afforded the same non-disclosing courtesy as before.

Not saying Amy didn't experience some bad handling from triads, just pointing out the facts.

There are other stories, and even photographic evidence of triad brutality towards celebrities in Hong Kong and it's no light topic of conversation, it's deadly serious on a level we can't even imagine in the U.S.

Can you comprehend Angelina Jolie getting kidnapped by the Mafia and Brad Pitt beaten up by a gang of mafioso so they WOULDN'T make a 'Mr & Mrs. Smith 2?' Carina Lau was kidnapped by Triads in 1990, and photograped naked after she refused to do a film for the Triads.

Those pictures were released to East Week Magazine, which printed pictures of her half naked, much to the protests of the Film Community. They eventually were forced to close down because of the bad publicity from printing them.

It's a REALLY bad deal over in Hong Kong and with things having changed (the industry is more mainstream China now), I wonder if it STILL is like that...

**GHOSTLY VIXEN** 天師捉姦

**(1990)** opened 9 days before EGS (5/10) and did a nice HK 6.2 Million. It's a two Amy Yip horror movies back to back.

The similarities end there. This is another lame Wong Jing quickie that has Amy in the first 10 minutes and then she disappears for half the movie, only to show up in some really weak battle scenes toward the end.

She plays a Ghost who has to suck off 100 earthly men in order to reach immortal status (no, seriously), but in hot pursuit is a leather-clad ghost hunter (or whatever) that wants to end her, because she's apparently evil. WHY she's evil isn't really ever explained...or what her quest is supposed to accomplish, or... really what the whole point of the movie is, but...

Oh wait... she sucks the life form out of her men! Why'd it have to be in the form of a blowjob? Oh yeah, it's a Wong Jing movie.

We then have to endure 45 minutes of Nat Chan Pak-Cheung 陳百祥 as a bumbling virgin and his brother Charlie Cho Cha-Lee 曹查理, as they go through every cliche and bad joke possible.  I like a certain amount of bawdy humor, but some of it is ugly and not funny at all, even for a Wong Jing movie. (Okay, the hotdog taped to the side of his leg thing is pretty funny...)

Sandra Ng Kwun-Yu 吳君如 plays his arranged girlfriend who he has no interest in, and just gets abused throughout, but for me, she's one of the things that at least makes it mildly funny.

I mean, at one point Bill Tung Biu 董驃, comes to the rescue. Sheesh.

Amy really is wasted in this movie - as a sex symbol, as an actress, as a character... the film transfer even looks like crap. My least favorite, so far.

They obviously had no idea the level of media frenzy Amy would stir up less than 10 days later in her next movie.

**LOOK OUT, OFFICER!** 師兄撞鬼 **(1990)** was released in Hong Kong theaters on July 28th and ran for 18 days, grossing HK $12,128,944, thanks in large part to Amy's rising star? Or the start of Stephan Chow's rising star? Duh.

Stephan Chow Sing-Chi's 周星馳 NEXT movie ALL FOR THE WINNER 賭

聖 would be one of the biggest hits of the year in China at HK $41MIL and his GOD OF GAMBLERS II in December would be a close second at HK $40MIL (though Amy wouldn't get to be in either!). And that wouldn't even compare to what he'd end up doing in 1991 at the box office...

I give Chow credit for putting Amy in a couple of his movies!

Bill Tung Biu 董驃 plays a 'supercop' (no, seriously) who gets killed by some gangsters that stage it as a suicide. He has a problem with this in being able to get in 'heaven' and is granted the opportunity to go back and clear his name.

Young Stephan Chow, becomes his reluctant human help and it leads to the usual Chow goofiness, with Stanley Fung Sui-Fan 馮淬帆 tagging along as Tung's former partner and Chow's girlfriend's dad. His girlfriend is a cutie, Ah Yuk, played by Vivian Chan Tak-Yung 陳德容.

Lots of silliness, and bathroom humor, with minor action. I guess if you like Stephan Chow, you'll find it funny. I've warmed up to his comedy over the years, it's good fun.

Amy's part is again brief, as she plays a highly decorated high ranking officer in

the Police Department (and looks quite fetching in the uniform). When Fung tries to take credit for Chow's police work (which was aided by Tung's magic), Tung uses magic to put a lust spell on Amy. She aggressively goes after Fung, as the whole office watches through her office window, exposing her (bra covered) breasts.

When Fung can hold back no more he pulls her down onto the desk and at that point, Tung REMOVES the spell, and Amy lashes out, embarrassed. Amy really delivers here as cameo's go, and this was a fun one!

**MORTUARY BLUES** 屍家重地 **(1990)** is a Corey Yuen Kwai 元奎 produced (and starring), Jeff Lau Chun-Wai 劉鎮偉 directed, Sandra Ng Kwun-Yu 吳君如 horror, comedy quickie that's not the best or the worst of the seemingly endless number of Hong Kong movies in this genre.

An ancient curse from the past unleashes a vampire and a bunch of zombie-ish helpers on a present-day town, and Yuen, Ng, Sheila Chan Suk-Lan 陳淑蘭, Lowell Lo Koon-Ting 盧冠廷, and a host of others bumble their way through dealing with it. Lots of silly humor (the zombies can only be stopped by rubbing their butt), and the usual Sandra Ng funny facial expressions...

It ran for 16 days, and did HK $4.9MIL at the box office, and a month after writing this, I can't much remember it.

Amy is wasted here in a small role near the beginning, as a performer dressed in Geisha costume - her top gets torn off to reveal a white t-shirt underneath- and she again takes a <u>punch/kick to the boobs</u> (though I suspect it's not actually her that takes the physical kick), but the scene isn't really sexy, funny, or all that long.

Maybe 2 minutes of screen time.

1990 the year in movies finally closed out for Amy with **RAID ON ROYAL CASINO MARINE** 霸王花之皇家賭船 **(1990)** released in Hong Kong theaters on October 20th and running through November 15th, pulling in a decent HK $7.1MIL.

Bit of a disappointment as it's a sort of sequel to Inspector Wears Skirts 2. The same cast: Sibelle Hu Hui- Chung 胡慧中 now married and retired, Sandra Ng Kwun-Yu 吳君如, the much-maligned butt of endless jokes, Stanley Fung Sui-Fan 馮淬帆, as the bumbling authority - still in action while his wife sits at home, and our Amy, playing the role as only she can.

So Fung and Hu's character are married now and she's retired, so Fung is recruited to re-train Hu's class to be Super Women Cops or something, and Billy Lau Nam-Kwong 樓南光 is along as his assistant and comedy relief (he was the shower peeper from the last movie).

They train and then go on a cruise ship mission to infiltrate some bad guys.

Much like the last movie, Amy has some well-remembered scenes in this, most notably her red bikini scene about 40 minutes in. Why someone didn't think to put her in a bikini until 18 movies into her career is beyond me. She'd only have a few bikini scenes in her movie career, but they are ALL well remembered!

Her first scene is about 7 minutes in as she waits with the other members of her squad to take a chartered van to their training facility. The driver turns out to be a wise guy and while Amy is in the front seat he pumps the brake up and down continuously, bouncing the vehicle and of course, bouncing Amy's breasts up and down.

At the training facility, Fung berates them and in Amy's  sparring match with Billy Lau, we get the first glimpse of how

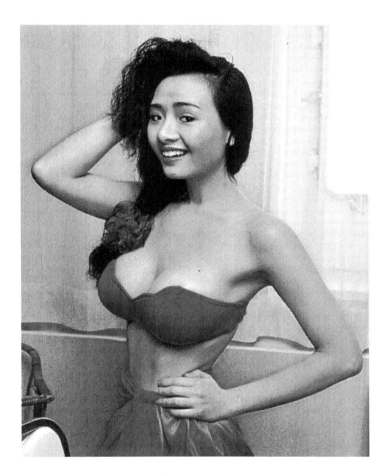

she works around her lack of fighting skills. By opening her top to expose her breasts (we see it from behind her), Lau gasps, and Amy punches him out.

Amy's charms are then used on Lau to get him to tell what the next day's training is. Unfortunately for the rest of the group she seems to enjoy it too much (make out session with Billy Lau - ugh!), so they break it up and then beat him up.

As punishment, Fung has them chained up to a metal fence that is connected to an electronic shocking device! Geez, what kind of training school is this?

Dressed in tight red tops and little white shorts, our Amy looks especially hot, but the shocks aren't real, as Lau has unplugged one of the wires. But when Fung discovers it, and casually slides it back in, REAL electricity shocks the girls!

On the boat, we see the ladies sun bathing undercover, and Amy's bikini of course. At one point she tries to seduce the Captain of the ship, but she can't seem to figure out the guy is gay. She pretends to faint (falling down the steps) and when he tries to give her mouth to mouth, she tries to stick her tongue down his throat! He's not keen on that.

Amy uses her boob exposure trick one other time, but the third time it backfires on her - she should've figured it out when the Captain wouldn't kiss her...

Oh, and near the end, Amy gets <u>a two fisted punch to the boobs</u>, and of course

Sibelle Hu comes out of retirement to save the day.

Lots of Sandra Ng in this one, but enough Amy to make it really worth checking out. I tend to like the movies in this series, and this one is pretty fun.

An interesting story from CINEMART (Sept 1990) *A yacht named Asia's Princess, frequented by mostly the rich, famous, and high rollers, is playing hostess to a group of star bright actors, including a sexy and breath taking 'Giant Boobs' of Yip Chi Mei.*

*GB is here on location for an upcoming feature film. As the crew of media reporters arrived to cover the event on this fancy floating casino, they were greeted by a tiny, red, hot bikini outfit, that barely covered our GB. This causes all the lethal cameras and equipment to take aim at GB's twin peaks.*

*Yip is well accustomed to the frantic attention that's being paid to her as she sways back and forth with her little waist and letting the reporters take good aims at her chest. Other actors were all but ignored by the press. To compete for attention, one actor yelled out, "Her breasts are the real McCoy, I've checked them out myself. They're not fake!"*

*His statement is in defense of latest rumors that GB's last film revealed uniform scars under her breasts fold. Upset by the rumors Yip allowed a male reporter to examine her breasts authenticity, and explained what appears to be scars under her breast was actually double sided tape used for support.*

I have no idea when she filmed it, but sometime in 1990, Amy returned to TV for a 10 episode romantic drama called **DESTINED FOR LOVE** (aka thirty eight beauty) 三八佳人.

Can't find a whole lot about it, but I lucked upon some screen caps, so enjoy! (Would LOVE to see this released on DVD some day!)

**EROTIC GHOST STORY 2** 聊齋艷譚續
集五通神 **(1991)** started off the year for
Amy on January 23rd and ran until
February 13th, pulling in a successful HK
$11MIL. Amy (and Man Siu) make a
cameo appearance here, but that's it for
them.

   And even though it's much more stylish
and beautifully shot than the first movie
(and sexual... a LOT of sexual stuff), it
lacks much of the simple charm of the
original. Really it's just an attractively
shot nudie feature.

   Chin King-Man's 植敬雯 underwater love
scene with Anthony Wong Chau-Sang 黃秋
生 is a real highlight here, and Charine
Chan Ka-Ling 陳加玲 is certainly fun to
watch frolic around naked, but for Amy
Yip fans, it's not worth it.

   It seems like both of her early 1991
movies were more favors to people she'd
worked with - Amy had her sights set on
bigger parts.

**LEGEND OF THE DRAGON** 龍的傳人
**(1991)**
on March 27th, was her 2nd Stephen
Chow Sing-Chi's 周星馳 movie, as the
comedian obviously saw the potential in

Amy for some funny bits (and physical charms). One of the top Hong Kong hits of 1991, it did HK $23.7 Million and ran for most of the month.

Even though Stephan Chow was nice enough to put Amy in a few of his comedies, this cameo, is fairly wasted. She's a shop owner when Chow and his brother visit Hong Kong (from their small town), and Chow is hypnotized almost immediately by the size of Amy's breasts, dressed in a modern cut leather top. Yep, that's about it.

We know how ya feel, bub, we're all that way, but can we get her a real role in the movie?

### At Last a Star!
## TO BE #1 (1991)
跛豪
Bo Hao

To Be #1 isn't the best or worst movie Amy Yip would ever appear in, but it was certainly her most successful. Pulling in an impressive HK $38.7 Million (about US $5 million!) over two months, it is Hong Kong's 31st highest grossing movie EVER, and the closest to mainstream commercial success Amy would ever see (it's a Category II movie).

By comparison, the 31st highest grossing movie in the history of the United States would be Star Wars: Epsiode III - Revenge of the Sith (at 10 times the domestic box office). Not that there IS any real comparison, the average big budget Hong Kong movie might be lucky to be in the US $100,000 range.

Note: At the time it came out it was the 8th highest grossing film of the Modern Hong Kong Era of movies - THAT's how big of a deal it was!

It IS derivative of many gangster movies in the U.S. - this is Hong Kong's 'Scarface', with Amy Yip sort of playing the Michelle Pffeifer role.

American Critics (i.e. Internet Film Nerds) were extremely divided on it, but in Hong Kong it won Best Picture and Best Screenplay, along with nominations for Best Director (潘文傑 Poon Man-Kit), Best Actor (呂良偉 Ray Lui Leung-Wai), Best Supporting Actor (鄭則仕 Kent Cheng Jak-Si), and....BEST supporting ACTRESS....葉童 Cecilia Yip Tung!!!

WHAT??? That's the wrong Yip!!!

Cecilia Yip IS really good in her part as the long suffering wife (the Diane Keaton-ish role), but make no mistake... Amy holds her own in this movie, looks great, and shows her acting chops.

Personally, I'm a big fan of this movie. I love Scarface, Goodfellas, Godfather 1 & 2... this is Hong Kong's answer to those type of movies and it's enjoyable. And it features one of Amy's most famous and revealing scenes...

Somewhat based upon the life of a real Chinese gangster, "Wuxi Hao', who DID NOT give permission to use his story, he nevertheless died shortly after the release of the film. It kicked off a 'biopic' craze in Hong Kong, putting Amy, once again at the start of another film fad.

It's the story of Crippled Ho, or Crooked Ho, depending on who translates it (Heck, one of the translations of the movie title is 'Lame Ho'!), who comes to Hong Kong as a refugee (sound familiar?) from mainland Communist China, starting out as a petty thief and working his way up to being the big boss.

Amy's part is a bit different from the usual role, as it's Ho's friend and chief lieutenant (吳啟華 Lawrence Ng Kai-Wah)

who falls for her. SHE just happens to be (Kent 'Fatty' Cheng) the rival boss' girl, which causes more friction between them.

Amy looks fantastic throughout. She looks high class and cultured, and only when the filmmakers PUT her into trashy situations, does she have to live up to that behavior. And boy do they put her into some trashy situations.

She's in bed with Lawrence Ng, when the rival gang bursts in and threatens his 'manhood', and later she has a scene with Kent 'Fatty' Cheng (Hey, it's the HK nickname, not one I'VE given him), where she is pledging her loyalty to him... well, I won't give too much away, but... the scene features probably the most famous side boob scene in Hong Kong history and one of Amy's most revealing moments on film up to that point!

We also get one of Amy's few Bikini scenes (out of 36 movies, only 3 or 4 of these knucklehead director's figured out to put her in a bikini?), and it is, of course memorable.

Unfortunately, she only has one dramatic scene in the movie (other than her humiliation in the Fatty Cheung scene, where her boobs get smacked around - no seriously, she is great in her performance in that scene), with Cecilia Yip as they cooly confront each other about who they are, where they came from and where they're going. I seem to remember it hinted they were sisters, but it could've just been the translation, as they were 'alike', which is a Chinese thing.

Amy holds her own in the scene with this Best Supporting Actress (nominee), and shows she's got just as much the ability to act as she does to be Hong Kong's most popular (at the moment) sex symbol. She fits in here as if born to be an actress.

Anyway, it's not the greatest and it's not the worst, but I certainly enjoyed it, and it appears that Hong Kong audiences did too.

Amy was a star now, she'd been in a huge movie, and she was poised for even bigger. Bigger?

May of 1991 was Amy's month at the movies with 4 different films playing, all in the second half of the month.

Combined they wouldn't draw as much as To Be #1 did, but one would end up being maybe one of the most infamous of her career.

It would NOT be **VAMPIRE KIDS** 殭屍福星仔 **(1991)** a small budget horror comedy hybrid that pulled in a low HK $2.1 Million over the 6 days it ran.

Again featuring Sandra Ng, 樓南光, It starts out with the group making their way to shore after their ship has gone down. Amy is passed out, so we get plenty of mouth to mouth and boob jokes right off the bat.

They find a diamond that awakens a monster, who sends Vampire Kids after the group. Ng and Amy wrestle over the Diamond, giving us some more wholesome fun, and <u>Amy gets kicked in the boobs</u> (there it is again). Subliminal message here?

The very SAME weekend, Amy was also in **THE GREAT PRETENDERS** 千王 **(1991)** with Tony Leung Chiu-Wai 梁朝偉 and Simon Yam Tat-Wah 任達華, playing an over the top gay man.

A little better, it ran two weeks and pulled in HK $4.3 Million. They also utilized Amy's picture in some of the advertising art, so they obviously saw the potential in that.

Also appearing is Joanna Chan, who you may remember as Blackie in **Jailhouse Eros.** Did she get a breast enlargement? She looks pretty hot here.

Amy plays it straight for the first half of the movie as a mahjong shark, and she

shows a deft talent
for comedy without
the need for any
boob jokes.

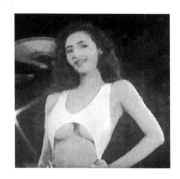

But then, almost
an hour through they
have some kind of
beauty pageant,
where Amy comes
out in a swimsuit that somehow, defies
the laws of gravity, and keep her breasts
in place. The judge takes a great liking to
her and she wins, but... of course it's a
scam of some sort in place....

Later she has a scene in her underwear
and pantyhose that is as sexy as anything
she's done.

Amy actually has a pretty large role in
this and is very funny. Worth a look!

### THE BLUE JEAN MONSTER 著牛

仔褲的鍾馗 **(1991)** came out the 23rd and
ran seven days, pulling in HK $2.6
Million. Not one of her most impressive
parts by any stretch, but it's somewhat
remembered for her outfit - a red
playboy-ish bunny suit.

The story, or whatever, is about a cop,
played by bit part actor 成奎安 Shing Fui-

On, who is killed in action, but brought back to life to catch the criminals, while keeping his pregnant wife in the dark about it...uh, yeah.

When he shows no interest in sex with his wife, she has a friend recommend Amy (I'm going by memory of an undubbed, un-subtitled copy of this movie, so bear with me), who is listed here as 'Death-Rays', to see if it's HERSELF that isn't getting him hot, or if he just doesn't have interest in sex at all. Misunderstanding ensues.....blah, blah, blah.

These three movies, that came out a week apart, still couldn't manage to do HK $10 million combined! It certainly kept Amy's... face in the public eye, and she was on a roll.

Her personal life was another story (more on that later), but for now she was a star!

# ROBOTRIX 女機械人 (1991)

**ROBOTRIX** 女機械人 **(1991)** may not be Amy's best movie, in fact it may be her most infamous, but it helped make her a bigger name in Japan.

It featured the equally well endowed 青山知可子 Aoyama Chikako (from Japan), and, unlike Amy, she has no problems fully showing them puppies off.

The infamous part comes from a pretty brutal rape scene between a male robot and a female prostitute, that wasn't a part of some cuts of the movie.

It did HK $5.4 Million, which is good for a Category III movie, and it did great business in Japan. Not only that, it was a monster seller on VHS in various cut and uncut versions.

It's the story of a crazy evil scientist who puts his mind into the body of a cyborg, and then goes on a murderous rampage. That rampage includes the rape of a prostitute, that's a very brutal and horrific scene.

He also kills, super hot policewoman (the aforementioned) Chikako, but HER brain is put back into a robot that looks just like her! Large breasts and all!

Performing this everyday procedure of the future is Super Robot Amy and her scientist/creator Dr. Sara (Hui Hiu-Daan 許曉丹), who's pretty attractive herself.

Amy's robot is just called 'Anna', but the new cop robot is called Eve-27.

So they decide to go after the evil scientist cyborg, played by Billy Chow Bei-Lei 周比利, but they get more than they bargained for.

He's apparently super, *super* stronger than the just 'super' strong female robots and he kicks some serious butt. If you're not familiar with Billy Chow, he made a whole career out of playing bad guys and scary thugs - he's perfect in this role.

The movie DOES actually spend some time exploring Chikako coming to grips with her robotic body. Her boyfriend, played by David Wu Dai-Wai 吳大維 (from Lost Souls, also with Amy) senses something is wrong and almost doesn't have sex with her, but she has a 'Hey'd you forget about THESE' moment and he changes his mind.

And STILL doesn't realize she's a robot. Proving that, when it comes to sex, guys are pretty dumb.

Meanwhile, the boyfriend, who's also a cop, decides that since the evil cyborg killed a prostitute, the best way to lure him out is with a 'woman'. There's a hilarious deleted scene on Youtube where the cops discuss going undercover as women, lamenting what has happened to them previously.

"I got both eyes hurt, plus a loin kick! I almost became a eunuch!" "Me? Never! I nearly got buggered by that Indian that loved gays!"

Very 90's Hong Kong comedy.

Of course the answer is much more simple than that, as Super Robot Amy decides to be the undercover 'hooker'. The problem is, she is so good at sex, that she creates a line around the block of men who want to see her! And when the Police Chief shows up...

The combination of humor, along with the horrific scenes, the Sci-Fi angle, and then mixing in the sexual scenes is exactly what makes Hong Kong movies so unique... And Robotrix serves up a good helping of all of it.

Which brings up another point: Chinese movies tended to be somewhat more shy about showing breasts than many of their other Southeast Asian neighbors, but Robotrix gives us a big helping of female full frontal nudity (from Japanese actress'). Were they specifically aiming this at a regional market?

It's also considered maybe the first Chinese mainstream movie to show (brief) full frontal MALE nudity. They were certainly pushing the envelope, even for a Category III movie, and even though this did decent business at the theater, it did BIG MONEY on VHS, where people could watch it in privacy.... One thing is for sure, everyone seems to be having fun working on this movie. It may not be art, but it sure looks like it was fun to be a part of.

According to cast member Vincent Lyn, "Now that was one wild shoot. The cast and crew were all over the place and you were lucky to find out what you were doing before the cameras rolled. I spent more time laughing on the set than anything else." *(from Great Martial Arts Movies: From Bruce Lee to Jackie Chan — and More, Citadel Film Series -2nd ed., 2001 Meyers, Richard, Citadel Press, p. 163.*

Adding to the slapstick, is 鬼塚 Kwai Chung, one of the police officers under David Wu, who mugs, goofs, gets bitch slapped by super robot Amy when he underestimates her strength, and even disguises himself as a 'john' to get a chance to sleep with her! He doesn't succeed, but rather is humiliated by her and the rest of the cops. (They've all been WATCHING the Amy performances on hidden camera!)

To say this movie has a little something for everyone's bizarre taste, is an understatement!

So we've got nudity, sci-fi, comedy, and violence; on top of that there's also some martial arts. Sort of.

Billy Chow of course has some skills, he's a male Chinese actor in Hong Kong, but that's about where it ends. Amy LOOKS cool, but the fights aren't exactly the focus of the movie.

Amy gets banged up pretty bad in one fight, and Dr. Sara has to make some touch ups, but then they all go back out to search and conveniently leave her alone in her lab.

Billy Chow's evil cyborg breaks into the lab and sexually assaults Dr. Sara, giving us more full frontal nudity. She may be in her early forties, but she looks great... and then, we get our second rape. They certainly wanted to let you know that Billy Chow's character was NOT a good guy.

So now they're REALLY mad at him and the big showdown happens.

The finale is, as with many of these type of movies, somewhat anti-climatic, but there's probably not a huge amount of people who necessarily stick it out to the end anyway.

As previously disclaimed, it's not Amy's best movie, but not her worst... it is what it is, and if you like this sort of movie (or just not offended about such things), it's fun. I found it to be both sexy and hilarious. Maybe even a little more hilarious than was meant.

Also, as previously stated the internet nerds were all bent out of shape on it. The sexuality of course, the nudity most certainly, the inconsistencies with the 'science', forgetting that it is Science FICTION.

The 'good' critics, managed to sum it up pretty succinctly.

Damon Foster, the creator of the legendary Oriental Cinema Magazine in his offshoot magazine, Heroes On Film #3 (June 1996), summed up his review with "Stupid at times, not a great movie, but entertaining, that's for sure".

In Oriental Pinup #2's Amy Yip issue from the Fall of 2000, reviewer Kevin Collins wrote, "Though certainly not on the high-brow level of Sex & Zen, Robotrix pummels it's source material and its characters into so much pulp and motor oil that it can't fail to please even the most hardened Western customer." That's about right.

Stephen Chow certainly gave Amy her shot with a part in his next movie **THE MAGNIFICENT SCOUNDRELS** 情聖 **(1991)**, coming in at HK $16.5 Million.

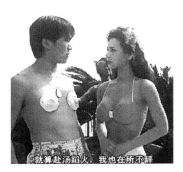

Already a star, Stephen Chow Sing-Chi 周星馳, would go on to be one of China's biggest comedic talents of the decade and one of their most talented film makers in their history that continues to this day.

He obviously saw the potential in Amy past just the big breasts, though make no mistake about it: her part in this movie is all about her breasts, but she is given a chance to show her comedic talents as well, and Amy shines and stars in this movie as much, if not more than anyone in it.

Amy gives us gross out humor, sexy humor, physical comedy, verbal comedy... she basically takes over the movie from Teresa Mo Sun-Kwan 毛舜筠, when she shows up at almost the half way point.

Side note: Teresa Mo performs a truly hilarious scene early on when she tries to scam Stephen Chow, who she believes to be blind... and plays the part of herself, an old lady, a dog and a police officer, inter-mixing them while trying to scam Chow...

Anyway, it's the story of a con man (Chow) who has to help pay back a debt and gets mixed up with another group that's also trying to run a scam in the same place.

Amy pretends to be the guy's daughter, so she can seduce Chow, who they don't realize is also running a scam.

It all centers around the suave loan shark, played by Roy Cheung Yiu-Yeung 張耀揚. A smaller role, of his brother, is played by one of my favorite legendary HK actors Yuen Wah 元華. He isn't given too much to do, but man oh man has he been in a LOT of Hong Kong movies.

He was Panther in Super Cop 3 with Jackie Chan, and the Landlord in Kung Fu Hustle - though he began his career as Bruce Lee's stunt double.

But hey, this is Amy's book!

So at this point you may have gotten the impression that I like this movie. I do. But really it seems as if the film makers are realizing that Amy has talents beyond her boobs, and has the charisma and acting talent to actually be a star...

If ONLY they would've kept giving her these type of roles in these types of movies... but life had other plans...

Oh, and I think she has a bit of a 'wardrobe malfunction' in this scene...

As fun and sexy as *Magnificent Scoundrels* had been **EASY MONEY** 老表發錢寒 **(1991)** starts off mean spirited by comparison. Near the beginning of the movie, Amy has a dance sequence, in which she is wearing a wig. She uses a

lighted standing shade to give the 'impression' she's taking everything off, but when she doesn't, the club manager says, "said to be nude every time, but lied to me still! I'll teach her a lesson!", and "You must die!"

It's a hot scene, until he starts off on that stuff. After the act, in the dressing room as he complains more, she says, "If I take them off, they'll soon be tired of, then no one will come."

He replies, "Susie, but if you go on with this, they soon get irritated, disaster will come then."

Yikes! Is this the movie or real life?

We also see: Amy cut her hair off! No wonder she had a wig! Sometimes it looks good, sometimes... well, it took awhile for me to get used to it.

So is the movie ok? Well, even though there's some negativity in that early scene, most of the movie's just goofy, and it IS Amy's movie mostly. In the cut scenes it looks like she was having a blast.

The problem is, the movie only did HK $1.3 Million at the box office. Which didn't bode well for Amy carrying a movie on her own. At least not a comedy. Or a Category II movie.

Was Amy taking a chance on an inexperienced director, a lessor known producer and a lack of co-stars, to show what she could do? If so, it didn't benefit her.

Next up, we change gear's completely with **QUEEN OF THE UNDERWORLD** 夜生活女王霞姐傳奇 **(1991)** a dramatic show piece for the Yipster that did a nice HK $7.3 Million in theaters there. Again she went with a lesser known director, but this was backed by the production of Wong Jing.

I may give Wong Jing movies some harsh light, but no question the guy was a machine who could pump movies out on a regular schedule and make money.

American nerd critics were harsh to it, but I love these type of criminal rags to riches stories, and considering Amy is the star...

Her performance is very good. For a low budget C3 movie, it's superb. I've read internet critics who say she's just eye candy in it, but they obviously didn't actually watch the movie.

Once again she has to show a wide variety of emotions in this, and she does!

Amy plays Helena, based upon a real Hong Kong Madam who rises from the bottom rung to being one of the most powerful underworld women in China. Ray Lui Leung-Wai 呂良偉, makes a cameo as Crippled Ho, from 'To Be Number One, in a great scene involving Amy's movie daughter Butterfly, played by Gigi Lai Chi 黎姿.

Like I said, I love these type of movies, and they move at a crisp pace, with ultra violence, sexuality, the passing of time, the characters rising or falling, and of course Amy!

Late into it, it gets dramatic and ugly, ending with a finale that is bloody, but somewhat unsatisfying, especially for a Hong Kong movie. I certainly would have done it differently.

But Amy proved she could carry a dramatic movie and get a decent showing at the box office. With the right script, the right director, the right production and the right marketing, surely she could put something together that would be memorable and prove to all of China that she was more than just a pair of 'Giant Breasts'.

Surely she could make a movie that would be remembered for all time...

She would. But not quite how she had hoped.

A lot was being made of Amy's new short haircut, which was first showcased in 'Easy Money' (Obviously she had shot 'QOTU' before it).

# SEX AND ZEN 玉蒲團之偷情寶鑑 (1991)

**SEX AND ZEN** is the one movie Amy will always be most remembered for and it is one of the most infamous in the history of Hong Kong films. At a time when Category III movies were considered a smash success if they did HK $7 Million at the box office, SEX AND ZEN shattered those expectations by pulling in a record HK $18.4 Million (Opening 11/30/91).

Sales of it on VHS and DVD worldwide are probably 10 times that amount, and it even got a premiere in California theaters.

Even though Amy has her usual amount of 'Yip Tease' going on here, the use of a nude body double, especially during the hot tub scene, led to a great deal of controversy and speculation (in Southeast Asia), and in some cases anger, as people seemed to be tiring of the tease...

Which is silly. Happens all the time in Hollywood.

Ultimately though, it would prove to be the perfect sex comedy, known throughout the world, and still in print on DVD and Blu-ray. If you're hung up about sex, it might not impress you, but other than that, it's an enjoyable romp.

It's the story of a scholar, played by Lawrence Ng Kai-Wah 吳啟華 (Crippled Ho's right hand man and Amy's love interest in *To Be Number One*), who marries Amy, only to find out she is not real keen on sex. A cold fish.

He travels, so he can fool around on the side, and one night he spies on a local silk merchant (Ayukawa Mari 鮎川真理), who is being abused by her husband. He watches them have acrobatic sex (and I mean CRAZY, FUNNY, acrobatic sex), but is dismayed at the small size of his own penis.

So he enlists the aid of a local private 'surgeon', played by Kent 'Fatty' Cheng Jak-Si 鄭則仕 (I swear this guy is in every other Amy movie), who transplants a horse's penis onto the scholar! Now he can make a move on the silk merchant's wife!

Lawrence Ng is funny and likable here, and Kent 'Fatty' Cheng is actually funny, but Ayukawa Mari in her only known role is amazingly sexy. Half way thru SHE is the star of this movie!

Amy, left alone for weeks by her scholar husband, has an interesting masturbation scene involving writing utensils, which is pretty hot and Isabelle Chow Wang 周弘 and Carrie Ng Ka-Lai 吳家麗 have a lesbian scene involving a flute (that's REALLY hot), but Ayukawa really steals the show at this point.

After Lawrence gets Ayukawa's husband to leave town in disgrace, he sets his next target as the flute loving Isabelle, and finds out she's turned on by the sting of a bull whip!

Meanwhile, it turns out Ayukawa's husband sells himself to Amy's family as a worker, and Amy suddenly is turned on seeing him chop wood while shirtless. Her vaginal writing must've awoken the passion inside her!

Lawrence also finds out Isabelle is into foot sex, food sex, and giving a hot bread

hand job, but when Carrie Ng breaks in and finds out she's been keeping him for her own... things get even stranger!

Then we get the famous hot tub scene. Maybe one of the hottest sex scenes ever on film.

Is it a bad thing that one of the defining moments of your career as an actress is a love scene? Think of it this way: Elvis Tsui Kam-Kong 徐錦江 is in two of the most acrobatic sex scenes in this movie, including one of the most famous ever, and anyone outside of China wouldn't even know him at all. Personally, if that had been MY only film role, I'd have considered it a great success! (Elvis Tsui had a long and respected career).

Amy has become famous around the world for this.

Don't get me wrong, I respect Amy's acting ability, AND her range as an actress more than you've probably read anywhere, but I make no apologies about her sexuality or beauty. Those who feel it is an 'objectification' or something negative, are just plain wrong. Do I objectify the sky if I love it for its beauty? Do I objectify a puppy if I love it because it's cute?

What is pleasing to the eye, or the heart, isn't a bad thing. Only when done in excess, or at the expense of someone else, can the admiration of beauty be overdone. (Which is a theme of the movie... sort of.... I think...)

All entertainment is based upon what we find pleasing to the eyes. If people can love action movies where hundreds of people die, why is it wrong to appreciate a movie of sexuality?

Ok, enough with the soap box... So, Lawrence gets pulled into a crazy, multi-person sex world orgy by Carrie Ng, while his wife runs off with Elvis Tsui, in disgrace, because he got her pregnant in the hot tub.

Years later, it all gets really overwhelming for Lawrence, and he looks terrible, like a meth head. He's goes to a brothel 'doctor', and because his eye sight is now failing he at first doesn't realize it's his wife, who was sold into it by her family.

I'm not a big fan of the ending, because of where Amy ends up, and then all of the male protagonists are forgiven by the local priests. What kind of message is that?

As well as the movie did in Hong Kong theaters (and other theaters around Southeast Asia) it fared even better on VHS and then eventually DVD.

In 1998 it got a theater release in San Fransisco. Now California has a large Southeast Asia population, so many

Oriental movies play in smaller theaters in different metropolitan areas.

San Fransisco Chronicle reviewer Edward Guthmann wrote *"The title may sound vaguely academic, but there's nothing even remotely lofty about ``Sex and Zen," a Hong Kong import that opens today at the Roxie Cinema. An unabashed soft- core sex marathon, much of it played for laughs, ``Sex and Zen" could catch on as a voyeur's delight -- an Asian spin on the jiggle- and-hump comedies of sex-satirist Russ Meyer (``Beyond the Valley of the Dolls")."*

Pretty spot on!

In reading this, I'll also quote him on a few things I forgot
to mention, like the director: *"Staged with zany abandon by director Michael Mak.."* and it's source *"Based on `The Carnal Prayer Mat,' an erotic classic from the Ming Dynasty"*

Amy had made her mark on Hong Kong Cinema forever with this movie, though it once again wasn't in the way she had hoped.

Some rumors have it, she was forced by the triads into making this film, and if that's the case it had to be even more of a disaster to see it succeed on the level it did. It would be the 2nd highest grossing movie (of movies she STARRED in) of her entire career and the one that the rest of the WORLD would recognize and remember her for.

Things weren't working out how she hoped and life was getting weird...

Amy Becomes A Pop Star!
## Running From The Craziness

Amy's whirlwind rise to the top included strange relationships, jealous co-star's, and a savage media that could not get enough of Amy, when it came to rumors and stories and pictures.

The Chinese media often wrote about Amy's relationship with Peter K.L. Chan, a Bank of America Executive at their Hong Kong Branch, that she met in 1988, while still in television.

Apparently he was infatuated with her, and as her career grew into movies, they became a couple (according to him). But it came at a cost. From the stories I've read, he sold his house and put his mom

*Amy Yip in concert. Taipai 1992*

into low income housing (despite making $3,600 a month - about $7,500 a month in today's dollars), just so he could keep up with Amy's financial demands.

With her movie salary, and rich boyfriend, Amy was able to accumulate numerous properties, including a two thousand square foot luxury villa (costing HK $7 Million), and live a lifestyle that made her larger than life.

But as her movie career exploded, the controversy with her boyfriend took a bad turn. In September of 1991, Chan was sentenced to 27 months in jail for trying to fraudulently transfer $2.37 Million (about $5 Million in 2018 dollars) into Amy's account from the Bank he worked at.

Reports said that the Police stated that Chan was 'obsessed' with Amy and her constant demands for money had driven him to commit the crime. As far as I can tell, she never made herself available for comment on any of this.

Was this what caused Amy to leave Hong Kong in late 1991, and move to Taiwan? Sure, she'd had rumors and speculation about her throughout her short movie career - everything from 'recording a message for a phone sex service' to the constant debate over the size of her breasts - but this was the real world now, and her 'boyfriend' was going to jail.

Another rumor was that newcomer Veronica Yip (no relation) was now the new Category III Superstar, baring all in two of her first three flicks; October of 1991's 'Take Me' 情不自禁, November's 'Hidden Desire' 我為卿狂 and then December's 'Pretty Woman' 卿本佳人.

Amy claims she left Hong Kong BEFORE those movies came out, but she could have heard the pre-release stories and knew Veronica was doing full nudity.

So she took the logical choice, and went to Taiwan to become a Pop Singer!

You'll hear conflicting accounts of how Amy's singing career went. She released her first and only music CD in 1992 to

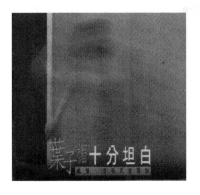

coincide with her touring around Southeast Asia.

When Amy had left Hong Kong for Taiwan in late 1991, it seems she had done so to try and wait out better movie offers. The Chinese film industry, which isn't exactly known for its special treatment of actresses, ignored it.

The press had a field day, of course, writing and speculating even more than usual about what was going on with her. Amy left Taiwan and spent the summer of 1992 vacationing in Hawaii. How could she show the movie business she didn't need them? How could she make them see she was a star?

Well.... she hired manager Wu Dun, and his idea was to make her a pop star. This isn't as silly an idea as it sounds.

In China, Japan, and Korea, many of the movie stars are also pop singers, including Jackie Chan and Anita Mui.

According to the September 19th Metropolitan Weekly, Amy earned Hong

Kong $10 Million for just half a year's work. She toured from Taipei to Las Vegas and really put the work in to try and be a star. But the Chinese press was relentless. In the summer of 1992 a magazine printed pictures of Amy showing her breasts pressed against a table while she was eating, what they claim is 'proof' her breasts are fake. Amy remained... eh... firm in her position they are real.

The Controversial "implant" photos which caused an Amy Yip fit

In her defense, actresses and reporters have 'felt' them and all have stated they were real. And none of her love scene co-stars have ever made a contrary statement either. It strained Amy's relationship with the HK press even more.

## Lethal Contact (1992)
龍貓燒鬚

Amy's next film, Lethal Contact came out in January of 1992. Running 8 days and grossing an 'ok' HK $2.2 Million. It looks like it was shot early in 1991, before Amy's haircut. Coming off the success of Sex and Zen it's disappointing. And probably green lighted because of that success.

The headline star of the movie is Kent "Fatty' Cheng, and it's yet another mindless juvenile comedy, and Amy's part in it is pretty useless; so I'm guessing that's exactly why it was released.

Amy is reduced to just a few minutes of screen time as one of two 'roommates' to the two goofy cops. Her one real scene isn't sexy or funny. And she's featured prominently on the DVD cover! Very, very disappointing.

With Jeff Falcon as the bad guy (dressed in full drag in one fight scene), and Billy Lau Nam-Kwong 樓南光 and Sibelle Hu Hui-Chung 胡慧中 playing their usual characters, it's actually somewhat entertaining at times, thanks to fights directed by Tony Leung Siu-Hung 梁小熊. Cheng and Lau were the primary directors.

But the lack of use for Amy in the movie is unforgivable, so this is probably one of the least likely re-watches on the list.

Three months later, we got **Stooges in Hong Kong** 不文騷 **(1992)**, a mish-mash of homages to American Comedy, that did an impressive HK $7.7 million, somewhat based upon a scene near the end where Amy's character gets her top ripped open and a full

frontal breast view. With electrical tape over her nipples, of course.

Amy plays the sexually frustrated wife of a comedian, and she looks great!

Her short hair looks stylish, and her clothing done fashionably. She is on board with the boob jokes, playing up her image, and seeming to have fun, and her

dildo scene is kinda funny. Most of the
humor is juvenile and stupid, but it has its
moments. They also do a 'freeze' scene in
the credits as a homage to Zucker, Zucker,
and Abrahms, with Amy, that I also
thought was funny.

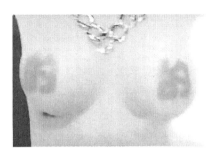

Oh, and Amy's
not really
topless (top pic),
that's some kind
of prosthetic
breast piece. The
close up though,
looks like real
boobage, but was probably shot on a
closed set without the crowd of people. In
the close up the camera specifically scans
down from her face to try and show it
really is her.

Even though the movie does focus on
her breasts and sexuality pretty
exclusively, it has fun with it, and Amy
plays it up well. Worth it for that scene
alone!

But in many ways, this may have been
the movie that ended the fascination that
audiences had for her. Not a whole lot
was made of the fact that she used a
prosthetic breast piece to 'pretend' to

show her breasts in a scene - it's actually a pretty amazing piece of art imitating life, or at least how Amy probably felt.

It was though, for all intents and purposes, the end of her run of successful movies. She wasn't wrong to make fun of her public persona and satirize it in a movie, but the reaction to it seemed to be harsh - Chinesee audiences just didn't seem interested in her acting ability.

If Amy had continued on... she might have eventually made her way. But with few roles available and the Press still hounding her... it probably just didn't seem worth it to her.

Amy also had extremely brief appearances in **Lucky Way (1992)** 大八卦 (which I've never seen) and **The Prince of Temple Street (1992)** 廟街十二少 (lasting about a minute).

It appears Amy was holding out for movies where she could actually act, and not just be exploited... problem is the studios went out of their way to exploit her anyway.

It's pretty clear that Sex and Zen had been a final straw for her, and she tried to be much more selective about the roles she took, even leaving Hong Kong during that time.

But the offers were few and far between, and what they pay a Hong Kong actress, even one who'd stirred up as much interest as Amy, is nowhere near the level of lifestyle she'd enjoyed up to that point.

After these next two movies, she'd need a new way of life.

## Those Look Yummy!

Sometime during her heyday, some restaurant got the bright idea to name a Pau after Amy and put it on the menu. Just to be cheeky, they made it a 'jumbo' Pau. Pau's are a fluffy bread with a hollow inside, filled with meat, veggies, or whatever, and look, unopened, a bit like a large breast pointing upward on your plate.

Try one, they're great! (Unfortunately I don't think there are any Chinese Pau royalties for name usage!)

<u>Falling star</u>
**China Dolls (1992)**
特區愛奴

Here's the best example of Amy vs the Hong Kong movie industry there is: A character driven story surrounded by exploitation.

Originally I saw a cut version of this film and thought, it was a fairly serious drama, featuring some fine acting by Amy. Included in that was a heart

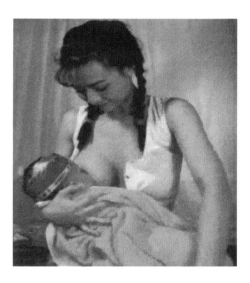

wrenching final scene as she sees her son with his adoptive family as they drive past her, in what will be most likely be her final time ever seeing him. I've always thought Amy had a certain sadness in her eyes; when she starts to sob, it really tugged at my heart.

I thought, "That's not a bad little drama", but I knew something was wrong because there was no breast feeding scene that the movie known for!

Anyway, when I saw the UNCUT version of this film, everything was still there, but.... holy moly, they should use these two versions in film school to show exactly how to turn a movie into an exploitation flick. Amy of course, stays fairly tame in that regard, but she does get creative with the 'Yip Tease' once again, covering up through the use of a baby's head as it breast feeds. Beyond that, this movie may be one of the reason's she quit the business all together.

Exploitation movies can be entertaining, no question I've been entertained by them over the years - but this movie just seems to enjoy showing you the abuse. Maybe it's the contrast with the story, which tries to tell a touching tale; either way, I just found the movie to be unenjoyable to watch.

Trying to make as much out of the part as she can, and certainly succeeding in that final scene, Amy herself takes some ugly abuse throughout.

She plays May, just a typical small town mother who is breast feeding her baby one night, when one of the members of her husband's party spies on her thru a window and then decides to try and rape her.

The husband barges in and at first blames Amy - smacking her across the face - but then ends up killing the attacker, putting him and his wife and baby on the run.

They're not on the run for long as the husband shoots an officer, but is gunned down by another. Amy is separated from her son and ends up in a training camp of sorts for working girls. In a large jail cell, the women are hosed down, until they submit to work for the men. Amy holds out until the very last, but accepts the profession as her only way to make enough money to find her son again.

Now of course they're welcome to a hot shower and the scene that follows (though Amy shows only her head and shoulders), has a lot of tough talk amongst the women, but Amy's purpose is clear - her son.

We get some amusing scenes of weird goings on of the working girl business, to try and humanize it, I guess, but it doesn't last long.

The really tough scene to watch is Amy getting chastised by her boss for not following the program, and wanting to be free to find her son. They hold her down and he smacks and kicks her boobs with his feet. Ugh. The glamorous life of a Hong Kong actress.

So it comes down to it, that she can't get her son back, she goes through years of this whole ordeal, but she gets to FINALLY see him, one last time, as he rides off with his adoptive family, and she breaks down in tears.

It's not a great movie, and not even a good exploitation movie, though if you like it rough there's some material here for you. But rather than paint an ugly picture of the underground sex traffic trade and how disgusting it really is, it really just shows the Hong Kong movie business and how disgusting IT can be.

## And then...
## Yiptease (1992)

Yiptease was a VHS release from Amy, that was put together to cash in on her celebrity. I don't mean that in a bad way, as really, it was somewhat ahead of it's time for a female celebrity to try and exploit her own marketability. But... this is really lame.

It's a series of vignettes; Amy getting ready, Amy and friends frolicking on the beach, etc..a lot of it slowed down and set to music that sounds like it was rejected from a Michael McDonald album.

Then we get Amy performing Janet Jackson's 'Black Cat' in concert. Not a superior performance.

It's not all that revealing, not all that exciting, and not all that long... some say it's a hour, it's more like 40 minutes.

It probably made Amy a pretty paycheck back then, but it didn't make her fanbase happy at all.

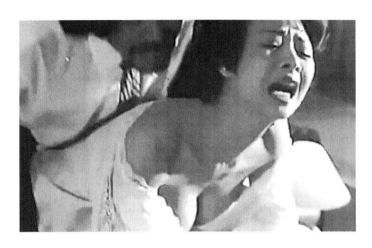

## Limited Roles
**Requital (1992)**
五湖四海

    Amy was limited to the type of roles she could play, but she had gotten box office results when she played those roles in films where the theme revolved around gangsters. If you're going to play a prostitute or an abused woman in a movie, I guess do it within a genre that'll have some success.

    But the Hong Kong market was crowded with gangster movies, and Requital wasn't exactly a great one anyway. Opening in late November of

1992, it grossed only HK $1.7 million and was out of the theaters in less than 7 days. This was actually one of the harder movies for me to locate, as I'm sure the lack of demand probably reduced production.

1992 was a big year for the Hong Kong film industry and Stephen Chow, Jackie Chan, and Jet Li all had multiple movies to crowd the marketplace. John Woo (Hard Boiled) and Ringo Lam (Full Contact) also released big films and even though Category III movies were on the decline, Wong Jing's Naked Killer made most of the headlines.

Even more baffling is that the movie didn't really use Amy in its promotion. She doesn't appear on the movie poster, and despite a really good performance, it just wasn't seen by enough people to make a difference. Realistically, Amy was the biggest star in the movie, and they completely whiffed on it.

Sure there's Lo Lieh, and an appearance from Jimmy Yang Yu, but those guys weren't even the stars of the movie, just appearing as henchmen. I wasn't really interested in any of the characters. Especially after the MAIN character rapes the only girl who'd ever been nice to him when he was young! It's not a horrible movie, it's just not all that great. It's a one time deal.

Worth seeing for Amy's standout performance, if you can find it.

She has her dramatic scene in it, but Amy could just as easily be lamenting her feelings on being a woman in the Hong Kong film industry. The one nice thing about this movie is it actually gave Amy a dramatic scene like this, instead of just using her as a pretty prop in another in a long line of male dominated machismo movies.

Having said that, after so many movies, where she ALMOST gives us a peek and teases us and teases us, Amy finally gave the audience what they wanted to see.

Granted, it was in a movie not many people saw, and it happened in a scene where you needed slow motion to catch it, but... there it is.

Yep. After all of these years of the Yip Tease...

<u>And just like that....</u>
## Amy accidentally flashes the camera!

When the gangsters break into her home to attack Tung (Tuo Tsung-Hua 庹宗華), the bad guy decides to bend Amy over the table and rape her (About the 32 minute mark).

It features one of the few stills of Amy from the movie, released and passed around the internet, showing her jiggling while screaming in terror (see two pages over). It was after the movie had already been released and gone from the theaters that I saw the still.

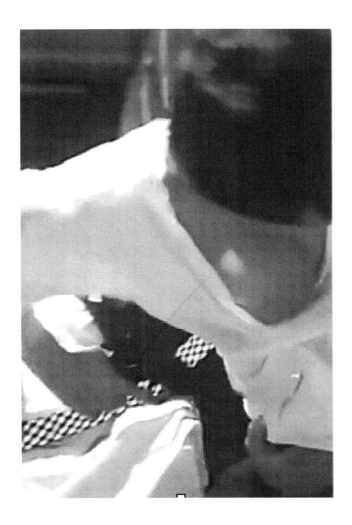

Of course, watching this movie many years later, and thanks to the ability to frame by frame go through it, I find THIS frame. And when turned at an angle...

When Amy reaches for the rapist's gun, she turns at an angle and her already generously exposed bosom comes into full view!

Was this Amy allowing it to happen quietly to see if anyone would even notice? If so, no one HAS until ME ... And that wasn't even the ONLY scene...

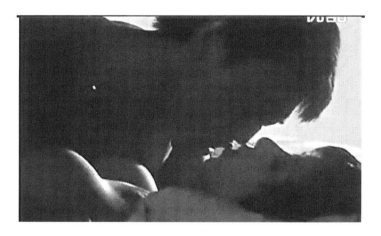

Going back to an earlier scene (About the 19 minute mark), when Tung and Amy first meet... I wasn't sure at first, but turning up the exposure and that looks like an areola....

Was Amy not getting the modesty that director's once afforded her? Or was she allowing it...?

Was this truly her last movie and way of saying, "Oh well, here ya go!" If it was, it wasn't exactly announced or talked about.

Amy's competition had turned up the heat and she was probably still facing pressure. It just became more than she was interested in dealing with. And she felt she had other options...

<u>Swan Song</u>
## Underground Judgement (1994)
地下裁决

Amy had gone to Taiwan (which generally tends to be a lot more celebrity friendly) and for the next year, all of 1993, didn't have a movie out at the theater.

Which is probably a good thing as the market was crowded, BUT she also missed out on the possibility to capitalize one more time on her fame.

Besides the usual couple of Jackie Chan films (City Hunter, and Crime Story), there was a flurry of Jet Li films (Fong Sai Yuk I and II, Once Upon a Time In China III, Kung Fu Cult Master, Tai Chi Master, and Last Hero In China) . Then you add in the Stephen Chow films (Fight Back to School III, Mad Monk and Flirting Scholar) and a final flurry of Category III movies, led by Wong Jing's Naked Killer follow up 'Raped By An Angel' and you can see the HK Film market was a wee bit crowded.

That doesn't even take into account something Hong Kong did 3 times more elaborate as the U.S. market, 25 years earlier. They took not one, not two, but THREE of their biggest female stars and put them together as SUPERHEROES starring in their own movie, AND released a sequel the same year!

I'm of course talking about Michelle Yeoh, Maggie Cheung, and Anita Mui in 'The Heroic Trio' and then 'The Executioners,' as Invisible Girl, Thief Catcher, and Wonder Woman.

So after all of that in 1993, Amy returned in 1994 with Underground Judgement. Now most likely this film was held back from the crowded market for at least some amount of time. Amy's hair style is consistent with her last couple of movies, and though it might look like 2 years had passed in numbers, her last two films were only 12 months apart.

Still, for a celebrity who was in the spotlight constantly there for a couple of years, it must have seemed like an eternity. So would the movie going public welcome her new film back with open arms (and open wallets)?

She has a scene as a wedding bride who gets sexually assaulted by gangsters in front of her husband at the reception and then... good roles sure are hard to find...

A tough movie to track down, because it sucks, and Amy isn't in it for more than 7 minutes. Waste of time.

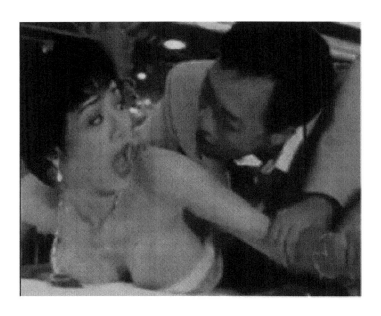

**AMY YIP FILMOGRAPHY**

Underground Judgement 地下裁決 (1994) … Ling

Requital 五湖四海 (1992)… Sister Yin

The Prince Of Temple Street 廟街十二少 (1992) … Asia (cameo)

Lucky Way 大八掛 (1992) …(cameo)

Stooges in Hong Kong 不文騷 (1992) … May

Lethal Contact 龍貓燒鬚 (1992) …Mimi

Yiptease (1992) … herself

China Dolls 特區愛奴 (1992) …May

Sex And Zen 玉蒲團之偷情寶鑑 (1991) … Yu Xiang

Queen Of The Underworld 夜生活女王霞姐傳奇 (1991) …Helena Wong Ha

Easy Money 老表發錢寒 (1991) …Susie Yip

Magnificent Scoundrels 情聖 (1991) … Apple

Robotrix 女機械人 (1991) …Anna

Blue Jean Monster 著牛仔褲的鍾馗 (1991) … Death Rays (cameo)

The Great Pretenders 千王 (1991) …Yip Mei

Vampire Kids 殭屍福星仔 (1991) … Buffalo's Sister

To Be #1 跛豪 (1991) …May

Legend Of The Dragon 龍的傳人 (1991) …
Boutique Boss

Erotic Ghost Story 2 聊齋艷譚續集五通神
(1991) …Fairy

Thirty Eight Beauty aka Destined For Love
三八佳人 (1991) TV

Raid On Royal Casino Marine 霸王花之皇
家賭船 (1991) …Susanna Yip

Mortuary Blue 屍家重地 (1991) …

Look Out, Officer! 師兄撞鬼 (1991) …

Erotic Ghost Story 聊齋艷譚 (1990) … Fa-
Fa

Ghostly Vixen 天師捉姦 (1991) … Pau
Hung

My Neighbors Are Phantoms 嘩鬼住正隔
籬 (1991) … Busty

She Shoots Straight 皇家女將 (1990) …
(cameo)

To Spy With Love! 小心間諜 (1990) …
Formosa 72

Jail House Eros 監獄不設防 (1990) …
Chesty

Doctor's Heart 救命宣言 (1990) …May

Lost Souls 富貴開心鬼 (1990) … Mimi

Mr. Sunshine 開心巨無霸 (1990) … May

Mr. Canton and Lady Rose 奇蹟 (1990) … (cameo)

Ghost Fever 鬼媾人 (1989) … Nanvy

The Inspector Wears Skirts 2 神勇飛虎霸王花 (1989) … Susanna

Heart to Hearts 三人世界 (1988) … Girl at Allex's Party

Who is The Craftiest 奸人本色 (1988) … Club girl

Heung Gong Ching 香港情 (1987) TV

Gung Chan 紅塵 (1987) TV

Bride With White Hair 白髮魔女傳 (1986) TV

Living Buddha Ji Gong 濟公活佛 (1986) TV

Gau Yut Ying Fei 九月鷹飛 (1986) TV

Cheng Mut Sei Daai Gei Neon 清末四大奇案 (1986) TV

Yin Ji Lui 胭脂淚 (1986) TV

Tin Ngaai Ming Yut Dou 天涯明月刀 (1985) TV

Saam Sai Yan 三世人 (1985) TV

Wong Chiu Gwan 王昭君 (1984) TV

# AMY'S MOVIE BOXOFFICE IN ORDER

1. To Be #1 (1991) HK $38 Million
2. Miracles (1988) HK $34 Million
3. Heart to Hearts (1988) HK $24 Million
4. Legend of the Dragon (1991) HK $23.7 Million
5. Sex and Zen (1991) HK $18.4 Million
6. Inspector Wear Skirts II (1988) HK $18 Million
7. Magnificent Scoundrels (1991) HK $16.5 Million
8. Prince of Temple Street (1992) HK $12.6 Million
9. Look Out Officer (1990) HK $12.1 Million
10. Erotic Ghost Story (1990) HK $11.2 Million
11. Erotic Ghost Story 2 (1991) HK $11.0 Million
12. She Shoots Straight (1990) HK $9.9 Million
13. Stooges in Hong Kong (1992) HK $7.7 Million
14. Queen of the Underworld (1991) HK $7.3 Million
15. Raid on Royal Casino Marine (1990) HK $7.1 Million
16. Ghostly Vixen (1990) HK $6.2 Million
17. Ghost Fever (1989) HK $5.9 Million
18. Jailhouse Eros (1990) HK $5.8 Million

19. Lost Souls (1989) HK $5.6 Million
20. Robotrix (1991) HK $5.4 Million
21. My Neighbors Are Phantoms (1990) HK $4.9 Million
22. Mortuary Blues (1990) HK $4.9 Million
23. Great Pretenders (1991) HK $4.3 Million
24. Mr. Sunshine HK $3.9 Million
25. To Spy With Love HK $3.4 Million
26. A Tale From the East (1990) HK $3.3 Million
27. Who Is The Crafiest (1988) HK $3.2 Million
28. The Blue Jean Monster (1991) HK $2.6 Million
29. Lethal Contact (1992) HK $2.2 Million
30. Vampire Kids (1991) HK $2.1 Million
31. Requital (1992) HK $1.7 Million
32. Easy Money (1991) HK $1.3 Million
33. Lucky Way (1992) HK $0.9 Million
34. Underground Judgement (1994) HK $0.3 Million
35. China Dolls (1992) ????
36. Doctor's Heart (1990) ????

## TOP TEN SEXY AMY YIP SCENES

Of course, YMMV but here is a tentative list of the Top Ten Amy Yip Sexy Scenes.

To be quite honest, I put this together off the top of my head, which is both impressive and a little bit creepy at the same time, but hey, I've watched 30+ Amy Yip movies over the last few months, I'm FAMILAR, ok?

10. Her outfit in **Blue Jean Monster.**

9. Ripping open her top, over come with passion in **Look Out Officer!**

8. Stripping down to her underwear and rolling around in bed in the **Great Pretenders.**

7. The love scene in **Requital** (NOT the rape).

6. Her 'love scene' in **Robotrix.**

5. The strip in **To Be Number One.**

4. The strip scene at the beginning of **Easy Money.**

3. The Scholar Love Scene in **Erotic Ghost Story.**

2. The Lesbian Scene in **Erotic Ghost Story.**

1. The Hot Tub Scene in **Sex and Zen.**

Is there any doubt?

## AMY YIP TODAY

Today, Amy Yip continues to lead a normal lifestyle, mostly out of view of the public eye. The paparazzi still follow her, and any appearance she makes to eat in public, or sometimes to even walk her dog, is splashed all over the pages of Chinese media.

She always shoots down the idea of a comeback, saying either that her restaurant business (in Hong Kong and Macau) keep her plenty busy, or that she's happy not having to use her breasts to make a living. And she doesn't miss the long hours of filming, traveling and publicity!

Amy is apparently still with her orthopedic surgeon boyfriend, Lim Kiam Hwee, going on 26 years. Rumors surfaced throughout that time that Amy was pregnant, that they were splitting up, that they were getting married, etc.

But everything appears to be the same as it ever was.

The one thing Amy has publicly stated was a regret that their weren't better roles for her to play in the movies, and one that she IS proud of is 'Queen of the Underworld'.

Obviously, by this book, I feel she had more to be proud of than that, and despite a film industry not exactly known to treat it's female stars well, Amy was able to make a name for herself and a place in the history of HK Cinema.

One thing for sure: Despite being a star for a short time, so long ago, the interest in her is still there. The internet has kept her legend alive and her movies will live on forever.

**THE END?**